THE JUNGLE

NOTES

including
- *Sinclair's Life and Career*
- *Background in Social History*
- The Jungle *as Propaganda*
- *List of Characters*
- *Brief Synopsis*
- *Chapter Summaries and Commentaries*
- *Characterization*
- *Review Questions and Theme Topics*
- *Selected Bibliography*

by
Frank H. Thompson, Jr., M.A.
University of Nebraska

INCORPORATED
LINCOLN, NEBRASKA 68501

Editor

Gary Carey, M.A.
University of Colorado

Consulting Editor

James L. Roberts, Ph.D.
Department of English
University of Nebraska

ISBN 0-8220-0699-5
© Copyright 1970
by
Cliffs Notes, Inc.
All Rights Reserved
Printed in U.S.A.

1999 Printing

Cliffs Notes, Inc.   Lincoln, Nebraska

CONTENTS

The Jungle Notes

SINCLAIR'S LIFE AND CAREER

Upton Sinclair's career is characterized best by the word prolific: during the course of seventy-six years he wrote dozens of books, pamphlets, and plays as well as hundreds of articles, speeches, and letters on every conceivable subject for a man who was interested in social conditions and social change. Estimates in the early 1960s give him 90 published books and 772 translations of these books in 47 languages and 39 countries. How many millions of words this output represents would be difficult to calculate, though in the early years of his writing career he was producing 2 million words a year.

His place in literary history is an ambiguous one. Judged by what has been written about him by critics and by his influence on other writers, he is a minor figure. Two of his contemporaries, Frank Norris and Theodore Dreiser, have a far more secure reputation on strictly literary terms. Sinclair is usually only mentioned in passing when the period in which he began publishing is discussed, like Jack London, a fellow Socialist. This minor ranking in literary history and criticism is partly deserved, because Sinclair invariably used the novel or play only as a means by which to convey his ideas about or criticism of society. This is ironical in light of the fact that he began by thinking his vocation was that of a poet.

Born Upton Beall Sinclair, Jr., on September 20, 1878, in Baltimore, he was the son of parents who were southern by ancestry. Several aspects of early family life influenced him profoundly. The family was poor as the result of his father's lack of success as a salesman, and this fact was set against the obvious affluence of his mother's relatives. His father looked upon the world of business as demeaning for a gentleman, and this plus his inability to support the family led him to drink excessively. Sinclair's abhorrence of drinking, apparent in *The Jungle,* was reinforced by the asceticism exemplified in his mother's life and opinions. Surely, this asceticism had a connection with Sinclair's later views on eating and fasting. Mention is made in *The Jungle* of a science of "clean eating."

When Sinclair was ten his family moved to New York City. Sinclair could have lived with his mother's well-to-do relatives, but he chose to go along to the city. It was only then that he entered school, and by the age of fourteen he was ready for college at the City College of New York. It was during this period in college that he began to support himself by writing hack novels. Most of these were about the lives and adventures of young men. Sinclair's views at this time were a combination of intellectual aristocracy and revolutionary democracy, and his self-admitted heroes were Jesus, Hamlet, and Shelley. He was beginning to believe that his true vocation was to be a poet. He received his bachelor's degree from CCNY at the age of eighteen, continued his hack writing to earn a living (by the age of twenty he was turning out 2 million words a year) and eventually entered graduate school at Columbia University. But his academic life as well as his writing for a living clashed more and more with the role of the poet.

In 1900 he left Columbia to isolate himself from the world so that he could write the novel he had envisioned as expressing himself as the true poet he had chosen to be. This he did do, and later that year he married Meta Fuller. His novel, *Springtime and Harvest* (later titled *King Midas),* was privately published in 1901. Sinclair's first child, David, was born that year, and by 1903 he and his family were living outside Princeton, New Jersey, in a shack and study he built himself. This was the first of several experiments in living that he was to take part in. He still had to continue the hack writing jobs to support his family, and this plus his newly found interest in Socialism began to weaken his commitment to the role of the poet. *The Journal of Arthur Stirling,* published in 1903, purported to be the diary of a young poet who committed suicide; it caused a sensation for a time until it was revealed as fiction, but it may well be a justification or explanation of Sinclair's giving up the poet's vocation. *Prince Hagen* also appeared in 1903; in 1904, the first novel *(Manassas)* of what was to be a trilogy of realistic novels on the Civil War was published. *Manassas* showed evidence of his conversion to Socialism, but the trilogy was never completed.

In 1904 Sinclair was commissioned by the widely circulated Socialist weekly *Appeal to Reason* to investigate labor conditions in the Chicago stockyards and write about his observations for the magazine. On a subsidy of $500, he spent seven weeks in Chicago living with workingmen in the packing plants and returned to Princeton to write the novel which he called *The Jungle*. It appeared serially in *Appeal to Reason* in 1905 and immediately caused wide discussion and reaction. Sinclair had great difficulty, however, in getting it published in book form. The first publisher he approached would not print it unless he made specific cuts in the manuscript. Four other publishers refused to publish it as it was written, in spite of the fact that there was great demand for back issues of *Appeal to Reason* from interested readers. Finally, Sinclair decided to publish the book himself, and Jack London contributed money to get the type set and plates made. At one point during serial publication, *Collier's* seemed interested but was reluctant to do more than print an article by Sinclair on methods of food preparation. Doubleday, Page and Company did agree to publish the book but only on condition that they could verify the truth of Sinclair's observations. They did so to their satisfaction, and *The Jungle* was published in January, 1906.

The Jungle made Sinclair nationally known and was his first book to be financially successful. He invested some of the income in physical facilities for a communal living colony called Helicon Hall. The idea of it was both attacked and ridiculed in the press, and after six months the experiment was ended by a fire. Later, from 1909 to 1912 he and his family lived in a "single-tax colony" in Arden, Delaware, based on ideas advanced earlier by Henry George.

During these years Sinclair published a number of books: *The Metropolis*, 1907, and *The Moneychangers*, 1908, novels on high society and high finance in New York City; *The Industrial Republic*, 1907, a Socialist view of America in the future; *Samuel the Seeker*, 1910, a novel; a book on health in 1911 called *The Fasting Cure; Love's Pilgrimage*, 1911, a novel described by some as of the same stature as *The Jungle*. When Sinclair filed for divorce but was denied it by the courts, he was invited to Holland where he lived for a time and received the divorce without any problems. While in Europe, he wrote two novels: *Sylvia*, 1913, and *Sylvia's Marriage*, 1914. They are notable for the believable portrait of a southern girl, and the second deals with the then shocking subject of venereal disease. In 1913 Sinclair returned to America and married for the second time; his bride was Mary Craig Kimbrough, a southerner and daughter of a wealthy banker.

In 1914, as the result of press silence on a Colorado coal mine strike, Sinclair staged a demonstration to draw attention to the plight of the miners. He was arrested, and he used the arrest to force newspaper coverage of the strike. He gave a full account of the meaning of the incident in his book on American journalism, *The Brass Check*. Later, he published a novel set in the coal mines, *King Coal*, 1917. Unlike most American Socialists, Sinclair believed his country should enter World War I. When the Socialist Party officially adopted a pacifist attitude toward the war, he resigned from the party. *Jimmie Higgins*, 1918, was a novel about the war whose purpose was to persuade anti-war Socialists to change their views. However, the final chapters reflect Sinclair's disillusionment with the administration of Woodrow Wilson, which he saw as betraying Socialism through American army actions in Russia.

Post-World War I years saw a characteristic outpouring of books from Sinclair: *100%: The Story of a Patriot*, 1920, a novel about labor spies; *The Book of Life*, 1921-22, a book conveying such wisdom as Sinclair had so far accumulated; *The Profits of Religion*, 1918; *The Brass Check: A Study of American Journalism*, 1919, the brass check of the title being the brass check used in brothels; *The Goose-Step: A Study of American Education*, 1923; *The Goslings: A Study of the American Schools*, 1924; *Mammonart: An Essay in Economic Interpretation*, 1925, which was called "social revolutionary criticism" of literature by a writer contemporary with Sinclair; *Oil!*, 1927, a novel based on scandals of the Harding administration; *Money Writes!*, 1927, a study of the integrity of writers in relation to sources of payment; *Boston*, 1929, and *Roman Holiday*, 1931, both novels, the first of which is based on the Sacco-Vanzetti case. Sinclair also wrote plays; *Singing Jailbirds*, 1924, is an example. It was based on incidents involving the IWW (International Workers of the World). The year before, Sinclair joined with the IWW in a demonstration for free speech and was arrested for reading excerpts from the Constitution.

Much of his life Sinclair had to publish his own books, until the time of the Lanny Budd series of novels in the 1940s and 1950s brought out by the Viking Press. He usually lost money on them, though orders in small numbers came to him steadily over the years. Some of his pamphlets were published by Haldemann-Julius in Girard, Kansas, publishers of *Appeal to Reason*. He encouraged their publication of inexpensive paperbacks ("little blue books") in a time long before paperback publishing became big business after World War II. Sinclair also assisted in establishing the Vanguard Press for the purpose of issuing cheap editions of books.

A frequent candidate for public office, he never won an election. In California, where he lived most of his adult life, he ran as a Socialist candidate for the House in 1920, the Senate in 1922, and governor in 1926 and 1930. In 1934, he ran for governor as a Democrat and was narrowly defeated by the Republican candidate. His platform was given the slogan EPIC (End Poverty in California) and was essentially Socialist in nature. He remained a Democrat in party affiliation thereafter but continued to support his own Socialist views. He produced many publications on both the EPIC platform and on his seeking and losing the governorship.

In 1932 he was nominated for the Nobel Prize, though he did not get it, and published an autobiography called *American Outpost: A Book of Reminiscences*. Other works followed: *Co-op*, 1936, a novel about communal living; *Little Steel*, 1938, a novel about industrial turmoil in the steel industry; *The Flivver King: A Story of Ford-America*, 1937. In 1940 he began publishing a series of novels using the central character of Lanny Budd. The purpose of the series, which ran to eleven volumes by 1953, was to present a "fictionalized world history of the turbulent period from 1913-1949," as one critic put it. One of these novels, *Dragon's Teeth*, 1942, won the Pulitzer Prize for fiction in 1943. Its subject was the rise of Nazism in Germany.

Later works included the following: *My Lifetime in Letters*, 1960, a selection of letters Sinclair received during his life; and *The Autobiography of Upton Sinclair*, 1962. After the death of his second wife, he married Mary Elizabeth Willis in 1961. In the last few years of his life any mention of Sinclair in the press made it sound as if he should have died long ago. This is the unfortunate fate of well known men who lead very long lives. Upton Sinclair died on November 25, 1968, at the age of ninety.

BACKGROUND IN SOCIAL HISTORY

From the point of view of history, *The Jungle* is both a comment on and a product of its times. And those times, of course, must be viewed in relation to what came before. The last half of the nineteenth century saw the making of great industries and great fortunes. Insofar as the relationship between business and government was concerned, it was a time of laissez-faire, with government providing consent without direction to a climate which allowed social change to be equivalent to business growth. The effective end of the physical frontier in America during this same period lent credence to the idea that industrial development, virtually by any means, was the next frontier. But the characteristic urge of Americans to pioneer led in a direction contrary to this headlong surge of business opportunity: to a series of Populist and reform movements which represented a desire to examine the social as well as political values created by a business-dominated society. If, as Calvin Coolidge said in the 1920s, "the business of America is business," what did this mean for individuals, their rights and expectations?

The conflicting directions of uninhibited business activity and individual political rights resulted, at the turn of the century, in a phenomenon called muckraking. Exposé for the sake of sensation became a serious concern for the sources of power and influence as they affected the individual citizen, with an accompanying sense of moral responsibility to seek the truth at whatever cost. In fact, it became a profession for a number of years for journalists, writers, and others. The names of Lincoln Steffens, Ida M. Tarbell, Ray Stannard Baker, Thomas W. Lawton, Charles Edward Russell, and Samuel Hopkins Adams were as well known then as those of Drew Pearson and Ralph Nader are now. They were investigators and crusaders, with more areas to investigate than time and energy permitted. A number of aspects of business and government were looked into and exposed. Publicity of this kind forced some remedial actions as well as some corrective legislation. A group of magazines became identified as vehicles for the muckrakers, and their circulation was some measure of the interest and concern of the American public.

Immediately preceding the intensified investigation of the meat packing industry, muckrakers were focusing on patent medicines. The impetus for this came from Dr. Harvey W. Wiley, chief chemist for the Department of Agriculture, whose research and experiments brought about the introduction of the Pure Food and Drug Bill in the Senate in 1902. Though not passed, it was re-introduced in the Senate in 1905 largely as the result of a series of articles in *The Ladies Home Journal* and *Collier's*, especially one by Samuel Hopkins Adams (published in book form as *The Great American Fraud*). The bill was stalled in the House in early 1906, at the time when *The Jungle* appeared as a book.

By this time, muckrakers were turning their attention to the meat packing industry, though the role of newspapers in this investigation was often compromised by the fact that many had large income from meat industry advertising. A magazine series on the economic aspects of the Beef Trust incidentally aroused public ire by revealing that the average citizen's assumption that meat was government inspected was unfounded. Inspection was a polite fiction perpetrated by the industry. Theodore Roosevelt, then president and earlier an active force in condemning the "embalmed beef" scandal of the Spanish-American War, responded to public pressure by appointing a commission to investigate allegations against the meat industry. The packers were exonerated.

The Jungle appeared in January, 1906, after serial publication in the *Appeal to Reason* the previous year. It is understandable that the reading public responded to details on meat production and plant sanitation instead of the conditions of workingmen or Sinclair's Socialist message. *The Jungle* helped to push the Pure Food and Drug Bill out of a House committee and to force Roosevelt to act. Roosevelt's response was to request the Department of Agriculture to send another investigating commission. Through additional pressure, including Sinclair's own personal appeal, Roosevelt agreed to yet another commission, this time of impartial social workers (Neill-Reynolds Commission). At the same time a Beef Inspection Act was submitted in the Senate, with Roosevelt's approval.

In reply, the meat industry managed to get articles published which defended present practices. Unable to successfully exert on the packers or Congress the pressures he himself felt, Roosevelt released part of the Neill-Reynolds report, which confirmed the essential truth of the way *The Jungle* depicted packinghouse conditions. Six months after the publication of *The Jungle*, the Pure Food and Drug Bill and the Beef Inspection Bill were passed. However, the first had no provision against false advertising; the latter was in a watered-down version brought about through the influence of the packers.

The aftermath of all this effort and controversy is interesting. The patent medicine and meat industries managed to destroy the Bureau of Chemistry in the Agriculture Department and neutralize Wiley's effectiveness as an agent of consumer protection. Sinclair was disappointed because the purpose of *The Jungle* was not even recognized. The problems which were supposed to be solved by the hard-won legislation persisted for years and years, and still exist to some extent now.

Virtue is often its own reward; and the muckrakers and propagandists focused public opinion but could seldom guide the course of its effects. If *The Jungle* as a whole is viewed as a propaganda novel, though it is somewhat like other muckraking efforts, it is ironical that it was in part defeated by superior propaganda from the meat packing industry. However, the fact that *The Jungle* could cause such a large industry to fight back powerfully attests to its own power as a persuasive medium.

THE JUNGLE AS PROPAGANDA

The propaganda novel is that kind of fictional work whose purpose is to persuade the reader to accept the author's beliefs on a specific problem or subject. To be understood, a propaganda novel should be distinguished from the novel in general and from those kinds of novels that most nearly resemble it (the muckraking novel or, later, the novel of social protest and the naturalistic novel). It is not easy to define a novel; and to say that it is a work in prose with a plot, characters, and a setting does not help much. The novel has generally been concerned with the difference between appearance and reality, from *Don Quixote* to *Portnoy's Complaint*. This is only to describe the mainstream of what is called the novel, though each age and each great novelist has redefined the terms on which appearance and reality are confronted.

The muckraking or social protest novel (respectively, early 1900s and 1930s) attempts to expose conditions which are thought to be inhumane or evil. To expose is, of course, to suggest change or at least to show the necessity for it. But to expose is not necessarily to outline a program by which change can be brought about. The most notable example of an American novel of social protest is John Steinbeck's *The Grapes of Wrath*. It vividly depicts the human consequences of the American depression of the 1930s but offers no program of social, political, or economic change by which the conditions depicted can be prevented. Sympathy for the Joad family is powerfully aroused, and the characters are unforgettable; but the reader is left with no alternative to the system which produces the plight of the Joads.

The naturalistic novel attempts to show how the lives of human beings are determined by biological and environmental forces over which they have no control and which they scarcely understand, on the assumption that if it can be demonstrated that these forces *do* control human nature completely then society can be reshaped and the knowledge of these forces can be used positively. The basic aim is the same as that in the natural sciences: from phenomena to laws to a more enlightened view of phenomena and an attempt to take advantage of the knowledge of laws. Examples of the naturalistic novel in American literature are *McTeague* by Frank Norris or *An American Tragedy* by Theodore Dreiser. In the latter, the path from Clyde Griffiths' childhood to his walk from a cell on death row to his execution is shown to be inevitable. Nothing can change this: not the ambiguity of the circumstances of his alleged crime; not Clyde's good qualities; not society's institutions of justice. Clyde is driven to act as he does; individual responsibility is meaningless. That being the case, as Dreiser or any naturalist implies, then society should re-examine itself and its relationship to the individual.

The propaganda novel is neither an exposé nor a demonstration. If it exposes conditions, it is only in order to make clear by what means they can be changed, to advocate the only kind of program (in the author's opinion) that can eradicate the conditions. If the propaganda novel shows human beings in the grip of forces they cannot control, it is only to outline those more beneficent forces that should be brought into being. Always the author of a propaganda novel has a program, a solution, the cure. His motivation for using the novel form is that this is the most effective way to promulgate his beliefs. Seldom is the propagandist interested in the novel apart from its use as a vehicle for his message.

The Jungle is neither social protest nor naturalistic. That its effect on contemporary readers in 1905 and 1906 was the same as that of a social protest novel is no measure of either the book or the author's intentions. Sinclair's oft-quoted remark about aiming for the heart and hitting the stomach is revealing. Readers took it for another muckraking effort, on unsanitary conditions in the packinghouses. Indeed, if the last three or four chapters are removed, it reads very much like a social protest novel. Also revealing is the fact that Sinclair was commissioned by the Socialist weekly *Appeal to Reason* to write the book.

Clearly, the purpose of *The Jungle* is to advocate Socialism as the only answer to the wage slavery enforced by capitalism. The book points out that labor unions have failed because owners can form even more powerful associations. The answer is public ownership of the means of production; in short, a radical restructuring of American society. Only by this means can the workingman gain freedom. There are no other alternatives offered; Socialism is the only way. Such, finally, is the theme of the novel.

Every fictional technique is affected by this purpose for *The Jungle;* every technique is meant to serve this purpose. Characterization, for example, is illustrative. The reader does not know the characters in the story any better on page 300 than he did on page 3. Once described, a character does not deepen or become more understandable. He is placed in the story in order to have something happen to him; what happens to him illustrates the fact that Socialism is the only answer. The range of characterization is small; that is, the characters all have the same dimensions, the same level of believability. There is little difference between the workingmen (largely immigrants) and the intellectuals depicted, for example, insofar as the way they are handled as characters. Also, characterization is entirely external: characters are defined by what they do or, more often, by what the author says they do or think. The processes of thinking, and moral choice are never shown. Intellectuals talk or, more precisely, have words put into their mouths.

Plot is likewise illustrative in *The Jungle*. What happens to the characters, even before the first scene in the novel (as revealed later by a flashback), describes the downhill path, with plateaus of false hope, of wage slavery under a capitalist system, a path only to be reversed at the end by the beginnings of a rise with the advent of Socialist beliefs. However, it should be pointed out that on the basis of events only one out of the twelve members of the immigrant family about whom the story is written is "saved" by Socialism. Events themselves are seldom presented first hand in scenes but more often in summary. Verisimilitude, in short, is sacrificed to the purposes of illustration. For plausibility, the author substitutes historical reference and documentation.

The use of historical reference brings in the matter of setting. Chicago, especially its meat packing industry but others as well, is chosen for its usefulness in carrying out the purpose of the novel. Its large industries based on an unskilled labor force; the presence of great numbers of immigrants; its political, social, and economic conditions from 1900-04 — these constitute a ready-made microcosm for an author with a message. (Almost the same period of time was used by Frank Norris for his naturalistic novel *The Pit*, published in 1903.) This setting is not invoked but rather used directly and often without regard for plausibility.

What this analysis of *The Jungle* as propaganda suggests is that it cannot be read with the same expectations as the reader might have in approaching the novel in general. The difficulty lies in being able to accept this necessity. Is a novel good because of its message, without regard to its use of fictional technique? The answer depends on the reader's view of literature.

LIST OF CHARACTERS

Jurgis Rudkus

A young Lithuanian immigrant whose "mighty shoulders," "giant hands," and dogged determination are virtually his only resources in the attempt to establish a life for his bride, her family, and his father.

Ona Lukoszaite

Fiancée and later wife of Jurgis, "a mere child" whose physical and emotional fragility allow little chance for survival.

Elzbieta Lukoszaite (Teta Elzbieta)

Ona's stepmother, who endures tragedy after tragedy with stoic acceptance.

Marija Berczynskas

Ona's cousin, an orphan; a young woman of immense energy, powerful body, and commanding voice.

Jonas

Elzbieta's brother, "a dried-up little man" whose satisfactions are a pipe and a meal.

Antanas Rudkus (Dede Antanas)

Father of Jurgis, an old man determined to pay his way in the family.

Stanislovas, Kotrina, Vilimas, Nikalojus, Juozapas, Kristoforas

Elzbieta's children; the last two are crippled.

Antanas Rudkus (Little Antanas)

Only child of Jurgis and Ona.

Tamoszius Kuszleika

An amateur violinist of more enthusiasm than skill who falls in love with Marija.

Jokubas Szedvilas

A fellow Lithuanian in the delicatessen business who introduces Jurgis and his family to Packingtown.

The Widow Jukniene (Poni Aniele)

An old lady who at various times rents part of her "unthinkably filthy" living quarters to Jurgis and his family.

Mike Scully

"A little Irishman" who is alderman from and Democratic boss of Packingtown.

Phil Connor

The Irish foreman of the loading gang at Brown's and one of Scully's political lieutenants; unwanted lover of Ona, and Jurgis's nemesis.

Jack Duane

Ex-college student and safecracker who befriends Jurgis and introduces him to the criminal world of Chicago.

Madame Haupt

An "enormously fat" Dutch midwife.

Freddie Jones

Playboy son of Jones the packer, with whom Jurgis spends an unusual evening.

Buck Halloran

An Irishman who is part of Scully's political organization.

Bush Harper

One of Scully's right-hand men.

A Socialist Orator

A "tall and gaunt" man whose speech profoundly affects Jurgis's life.

Ostrinski

A Polish pants-finisher and Socialist who first instructs Jurgis in his new beliefs.

Tommy Hinds

Hotel keeper and state organizer of the Socialist Party.

Mr. Lucas

An "itinerant evangelist" who becomes a traveling Socialist speaker.

Nicholas Schliemann

A Swedish ex-university professor and Socialist theoretician.

BRIEF SYNOPSIS

The wedding feast of Jurgis Rudkus and Ona Lukoszaite, Lithuanian immigrants newly arrived in Chicago's Packingtown, is celebrated in the traditional manner, with Elzbieta, Ona's stepmother, and Marija Berczynskas, her cousin, managing the event and Tamoszius Kuszleika providing the music. The wedding has taken place only after some delay, however. Earlier, Ona and Elzbieta are shown to have decided to come to America at the suggestion of Jonas, Elzbieta's brother, when Ona's father dies and leaves them with little money. Jurgis, in love with Ona, joins the immigrants, along with his father and Marija and Elzbieta's six children. When they arrive in Chicago, they are introduced to Packingtown by Jokubas Szedvilas, a friend of Jonas who preceded them to America. The family rents part of a filthy apartment, Jurgis gets a job easily, and they tour one of the packinghouses. Jonas and Marija soon find work, though Jurgis's father Dede Antanas cannot, and they feel the necessity to buy a home of their own. In ignorance and great anxiety, they do buy a house, only to discover there are many costs they are unaware of. Their increased expenses cause Ona and Stanislovas, Elzbieta's oldest son, to have to find jobs. The delay in the wedding of Jurgis and Ona is caused by the older members of the family insisting they wait until a proper feast can be paid for, but finally the event does take place.

Jurgis begins to learn of unsanitary conditions in the plants as well as the ruthless way in which workers are treated. His father does get a job, by bribery; but the conditions in which he works cause his death. The winter is cruel for all people in Packingtown, but it is lightened for the family by the romance between Marija and Tamoszius. However, Marija's being laid off postpones their wedding; and this time Jurgis, along with Marija, is eager to join the labor union. Jurgis becomes a citizen and votes in an election, now learning for the first time of the Democratic boss of Packingtown, Mike Scully. Jurgis is further disillusioned by what he sees at work and by additional costs on the house. Marija goes back to work but is fired for insisting on her rights. She does find another job but learns the hard lesson in Packingtown of hanging on to a place. Ona, now pregnant, understands this truth and continues in her job even though the fact that her forelady runs a brothel is repugnant to her. Her baby is born, a boy called Antanas after Jurgis's father, and Ona must return to work.

Spraining his ankle on the killing beds, Jurgis is unable to work for a long time, and this brings him face to face with despair. Jonas leaves unexpectedly, and more of the children go to work. When Jurgis is well, though not as strong as he used to be, he looks for work unsuccessfully and realizes he is no longer useful. Following the death of one of Elzbieta's two crippled sons, Jurgis is forced to take a job in a fertilizer plant, a place no man chooses if he can avoid it. When Jurgis decides the younger children should get off the street and no longer sell newspapers, Elzbieta herself must find a job. With the daily grind of work and so little income, all the family feel defeated, especially Jurgis, who takes to drinking to forget the conditions of his job. Ona, now pregnant again, is going to pieces in a way unaccountable to Jurgis. Then, several times she does not come home at all, and this finally leads Jurgis to confront her with her actions. She confesses to adultery forced on her by Connor, a foreman where she and Jurgis work. Jurgis condemns her and blindly attacks Connor, ending up in jail for the assault.

Unable to post bond, Jurgis remains in jail. The beginnings of a sense of injustice are reinforced by meeting Jack Duane, who introduces him to other inmates and to a knowledge of the sick side of society. Jurgis is cried and sentenced to thirty days. His imprisonment is made more cruel by a visit from Stanislovas with news of all the family problems. When Jurgis is released and finally gets back to Packingtown, he discovers the family has lost the house and Ona is in labor early. With almost no money, Jurgis persuades a midwife to come to Ona; but it is too late to save either Ona or the child. For several days Jurgis stays drunk but does return, to hear Elzbieta's pleas to pull himself together for the sake of little Antanas.

Blacklisted in Packingtown, Jurgis joins all the other unemployed who are looking for work. By chance he is able to get a
job at the harvester works, a factory whose working conditions
are considered a model of enlightenment; but he is shortly laid
off even as men are in Packingtown. He is about to give up when
a chance encounter between a settlement worker and one of
Elzbieta's sons at the dump leads to a job in a steel mill. As with
the job at the harvester works, Jurgis again feels optimistic about
the future, though he misses some time at work when he burns
his hand in helping an injured man. However, the death of little
Antanas, who drowns in the street after a heavy rain, destroys
that optimism. Instead of drinking, this time Jurgis flees Chicago
and spends the summer tramping around the Midwest, for the
first time free and able to enjoy fresh air and sunshine. He meets
others like himself and resolutely refuses to think about what is
left of his family.

But cold weather sends him back to Chicago. He tramps the
streets until he finds a job digging a tunnel for telephone lines,
though in reality they are subways for freight transportation. But
an accident in which his arm is broken ends his expectation of a
winter's employment. Out of the county hospital, he is on the
streets again, helpless. He tries everything: spending a little
money in order to get warmth in a saloon; going to a revival
meeting for the same purpose; trying to get into a corridor in a
police station for the night. At last, he is forced to beg; but he is
an unsuccessful amateur at it. However, begging does lead to an
encounter with a wealthy young man who, drunk, invites him
home to what turns out to be a mansion. He is Freddie Jones, son
of Jones the packer; he shows Jurgis the house and is amused
that Jurgis has worked in the yards. Jurgis is eventually thrown
out of the house, but he takes with him a hundred dollar bill
young Jones has given him. Attempting to cash it in a saloon,
however, leads to a fight, and he is in jail again. Sentenced to ten
days, he once more encounters Duane in prison.

When he is released, Jurgis goes to Duane; and they team up
for a life of crime, with Duane providing the knowledge of

Chicago's underworld. Jurgis also learns of the connections among criminals, politicians, and businessmen. He meets two of Mike Scully's men, "Buck" Halloran and "Bush" Harper, and through them gets into politics. He agrees to return to Packingtown in a scheme to elect a Republican alderman so that Scully can assure his own election unopposed the following year. Jurgis meets Scully, is given a job at one of the packinghouses, and successfully works for the election of the Republican. Afterwards, he remains in his job at the yards; and when the men go out on strike he is advised by Scully to stay on as a scab. He is welcomed back by his boss and is able to demand higher wages; soon, he is put in charge of the killing beds at an even higher wage. But the other strikebreakers are largely Negroes brought in from the South, and it is impossible to organize them. When the packers appear to agree to a settlement with the union but refuse to rehire union leaders, the strike is on again; and conditions in the plants are chaotic. There is little Jurgis can do, and he even assists in forays against the striking workers.

After one such occasion, he encounters Conner again and again attacks him. Though Jurgis has help from "Bush" Harper, Connor turns out to be one of Scully's men; it costs all of Jurgis's savings to get his bail reduced. He is free but penniless and out on the street again. Hunting a job is harder now with the strike, and when the strike fails and the men go back to work, the strikebreakers themselves are looking for work. Even when Jurgis is offered a job he cannot hold it, and he resorts to soup kitchens, stale-beer dives, and any meeting that offers warmth. By chance he locates Marija and goes to find her in a brothel. Jurgis learns of her life there and her prospects for the future, as well as her belief that Jurgis should have let Ona continue with Connor so the family could have been supported. Marija tells him where to find Elzbieta and the children, whom she is supporting. Before he goes to them he wants to find a job; to keep warm he goes to what turns out to be a Socialist rally. The stirring speech he hears makes Jurgis realize he need not be defeated and he can be a free man.

It is a moment that changes his life. He goes to see the speaker after the rally and is turned over to another Socialist

24

comrade, Ostrinski. Ostrinski explains the meaning of Socialism to him and the way this set of doctrines enables the individual to understand the truth about society, for example, the nature of the Beef Trust. It is a sober and industrious Jurgis who goes back to Elzbieta and is accepted. He gets a job as porter at a hotel run by a Socialist organizer, Tommy Hinds. From him and others, as well as from reading, Jurgis gains an education in the nature of American society and the way Socialism would change it. He is eager to convert others and impatient with resistance to his new ideas. He notices the effects the Socialist Party has had in Packingtown; with an election campaign in progress Scully and the Democrats are having a hard time of it.

A significant event in Jurgis's new life is an evening spent listening to two Socialist thinkers: Lucas, an evangelist turned traveling Socialist speaker; and Schliemann, an ex-university professor who has become a Socialist theoretician. From them Jurgis learns how Socialism could remake society into a haven for the free individual by removing the control of wealth from the hands of capitalists. The next day, the results of a presidential election (1904) show remarkable Socialist gains in Chicago and definite advances all over the country. At an election night rally, a speaker urges the assembled Socialists to consolidate the gains made and to work for the day when Chicago will be theirs.

SUMMARIES AND COMMENTARIES

CHAPTER 1

Summary

Following the wedding of Ona Lukoszaite and Jurgis Rudkus, a *veselija,* or wedding feast, is held in the back room of a saloon. The guests of the Lithuanian couple are from the stockyards area of Chicago, where they all live. The traditional affair is managed by a cousin of Ona's, Marija Berczynskas.

The feast is a substantial one, prepared by a number of women including Teta Elzbieta, Ona's stepmother. Amid much noise and confusion, the wedding party and the guests sit down to eat. The confusion is heightened by the vigorous playing of a trio of musicians led by Tamoszius Kuszleika. They play songs requested by the guests and also serenade the bride. The feast ends with the customary speech, delivered by Jurgis's father, Dede Antanas.

The musicians also play for the dancing which follows the dinner. Young and old alike dance, each in his own style. The main event of the evening is finally reached; this is the traditional ceremony of the *acziavimas*. It involves each man's dancing with the bride and then making a gift of money to help pay for the feast and provide the bride and groom with a start in life.

On this occasion, however, though the older people observe the custom of gifts, many of the young do not. There is much discussion of the way the young are ignoring old and treasured traditions in the new country. It looks as if the expenses of the *veselija* would not be met. Ona is sick with worry over the problem, but Jurgis characteristically says he will work harder.

As the dancers dance on and on in a stupor and a policeman keeps an eye out for quarrels, Ona and Jurgis leave for home, knowing they must go to work in the morning as on any other day.

Commentary

That Sinclair opens his novel with the scene of a wedding celebration is of interest for several reasons. It is the beginning of life together for Jurgis and Ona, the main characters. And that life is begun by observance of an old-country custom of the wedding feast. It is not possible for these immigrants to follow many of the traditions they brought with them; weddings and funerals are about the only occasions. The fact that this is so suggests the circumstances which they now find themselves in and which Sinclair tries to depict in detail throughout the book.

Though the celebration has much of the flavor of a peasant wedding—with much to eat and drink, with sentimental music

and marathon dancing—it is in fact held in a back room of a saloon in the stockyards district of Chicago. Little is said in this
first chapter of the lives these peasants-become-workers lead,
but the setting is enough to sound a discordant note. This note is
reinforced by the obvious "generation gap": the young people
do not dress in the traditional clothes, they dance in the current
American style, and many of the young men ignore the ceremony
of the *acziavimas*. And the older people lament this straying
from the old ways.

It is entirely appropriate that this opening scene should be
ambiguous in effect. Normally, a wedding suggests happiness;
but Sinclair has a grim story to tell and is unrelenting in the way
he goes about it. Also, unlike the usual novel, this one is intended to convey an urgent message by all the means at its dis-
posal. Events are important only insofar as they illustrate this
message. Sinclair uses the form of the novel only because it is
an effective way of getting this message to the reader. This is
revealed, for example, in the way point of view is used. Not
once does the reader see through the eyes or mind of one of the
characters. It is always the omniscient author; it is always Sinclair who is telling the reader to look at this; to notice that, to
think these thoughts, or to come to that conclusion. The author
allows no choice; the reader must see as he sees.

In spite of the discordant note in this first chapter, the peasant's joy in celebration is conveyed colorfully. The appearance
of a "great platter of stewed duck" and a "big yellow bowl of
smoking potatoes" signals the beginning of a crowded, noisy
meal, made even more confusing by the vigorous playing of the
trio of musicians. Songs are called for, and the music reminds
the celebrants of home far away. The dancing which follows is
equally spirited. A variety of costumes is described, as well as
a variety of dancing styles. Some older people simply move a
little to enjoy the rhythm of the music, while bold younger ones
careen exuberantly around the room without regard for others.
Not many such celebrations are held, and everyone enjoys this
one, even to the point of exhaustion.

In this noisy, fast-moving scene Sinclair places his main
characters, the newly married Jurgis and Ona. His portraits of

the two are static, perhaps appropriate to the fact that they seem so little a part of what is going on. And Sinclair says little about either. Ona has a "wan little face," is "blue-eyed and fair," is "not quite sixteen," and is "small for her age." By contrast, Jurgis has "great black eyes with beetling brows," "thick black hair," "mighty shoulders," and "giant hands." Both give evidence of being under great emotional stress, as would be expected on such an occasion.

But if the guests of honor are present in name only, Tamoszius and Marija are the active agents in almost everything that happens. Marija's is an action portrait. She has planned the whole affair and is everywhere to see that it goes as it should. She pushes the crowd this way and that as they enter the saloon; she gives orders in the kitchen and helps get the food served; she urges the musicians to play and teaches them a song; she oversees the dancing and manages the *acziavimas;* she keeps the celebration going long after everyone is exhausted; she even starts the only serious fight of the evening. To follow her is to be constantly on the move. When she is described, she turns out to appear almost mannish, almost grotesque.

Tamoszius certainly is a caricature. He is a man defined by only one attribute: his love for music. He is possessed by it, "inspired." That is his virtue. He is not a good musician; self-taught, he plays vigorously, not well. With his "wizened-up little face" and striped shirt and military pants that are too short, Tamoszius would be a figure of ridicule if he were not a musician.

Many of the minor characters are no more than stereotypes: for example, the bartender with "waxed black mustaches" and a "carefully oiled curl plastered against one side of his forehead" or the policeman who is fat. Others are given more depth, as, for example, some of the couples dancing.

Sinclair's range of characterization is rather small. There is very little difference between his handling of Ona and his handling of the bartender. The reader knows little about either. Here as elsewhere the author's use of the novel is heavily influenced by his purpose in writing the book.

That purpose is not yet clearly defined in this first chapter, only implied. In general terms, his purpose seems to be the depiction of the immigrant in the new world. Using the setting of the stockyards is appropriate since almost all of the unskilled men were then immigrants. It will turn out, however, that for most of the novel his aim is more specific: to show the condition of the workingman in the yards. This purpose is implied only in Sinclair's comments about the work Dede Antanas and Mikolas do, and about the necessity for all of them to be at work on time the morning after the wedding feast.

CHAPTERS 2-3

Summary

In a flashback, Jurgis's life in Lithuania and his meeting Ona are described. Raised in the country, Jurgis has little hope of marrying this daughter of a wealthy man. But her father dies, and the family is left with little to support them. They decide to go to America—Ona, Teta Elzbieta, her six children, and her brother Jonas, as well as Ona's cousin Marija—and Jurgis earns enough money to go with them and take his father. Though cheated of much of their money, they do manage to get to Chicago, where a friend of Jonas has gone earlier and is said to have gotten rich.

Lost in Chicago, they are finally put on a street car for the stockyards. They observe the desolate landscape and drab houses as they ride and encounter for the first time the peculiar smells and sounds and sights of their new home. Once let off at the yards, they accidentally encounter Jonas's friend, who is operating a delicatessen. He finds them a place to stay at the Widow Jukniene's, a dirty four-room apartment in a two-story tenement. The women will share a room with the Widow Jukniene and her three children.

Later in the summer afternoon, Jurgis and Ona go for a walk to look over their neighborhood. They notice the many children playing in bare lots and in the water standing in the dirt streets, the flies attracted by the fact the land is a former garbage dump. Not far away is the currently used dump as well as a large brickyard. The sordidness of the scene is less important to them than the power represented by Packingtown.

Jurgis's size and obvious strength easily win him a job at Brown's the next morning. He is hired to shovel guts. Jonas's friend Jokubas Szedvilas thinks he can get jobs for Jonas and Dede Antanas. Employment taken care of, Jokubas guides the family on a tour of the yards.

They see the endless cattle pens and the activity of buying and selling. Jokubas recites statistics for them and explains the operations of the railroads. He takes them into a building at Durham's, and they join a guided tour. A visit to the hog-killing operation is first.

They observe the hogs coming up the chute to the top of the building, the way in which they are chained by a leg to a wheel and delivered to a trolley, and the way they are killed. The carcass of every hog is handled by many men, each performing a specialized job. Before entering the chilling room, each carcass is supposed to be inspected by a government inspector. On floors below, Jurgis and the others see how the waste materials are treated, how the chilled carcasses are butchered, and how the meat is packaged and loaded in freight cars. "It was pork-making by machinery, pork-making by applied mathematics."

Across the street, they discover the beef-killing operation is quite different. It is conducted on one floor; and after the cattle are stunned by a sledge hammer and taken to the killing beds, they are strung up in as many lines, and the crew of men go from one line to another carrying out their specialized jobs. Jurgis and his family also see what happens to all the waste material and how the meat is prepared for shipment all over the world. They find, too, that Durham's consists of many subsidiary industries, all the way from a power plant to a fertilizer factory.

Told by Jokubas how many people the several packing-houses employ and support as well as feed by their products,

Jurgis looks upon the yards as "a thing as tremendous as the universe."

Commentary

The description of the "back of the yards" brings into perspective the scene of the peasant wedding feast in Chapter 1. The feast is a special occasion, a touch of nostalgia; the yards are day-to-day reality. Sinclair depicts the setting in all its seaminess, the result of first-hand observation. Colors are dingy; the landscape is "hideous and bare." But most of all these newly arrived immigrants are struck by the "pungent odor." "It was an elemental odor, raw and crude; it was rich, almost rancid, sensual, and strong." Then, too, there is the smoke: "thick, oily, and black as night." And the "ten thousand little sounds" of the animals penned up in the yards.

The streets have "great hollows full of stinking green water," and the former garbage dump has a "strange, fetid odor," a "ghastly odor, of all the dead things of the universe." And they are to live in a room of an apartment which is unspeakably dirty, as well as crowded.

Sinclair must have been especially offended by the smells he encountered in his several weeks in the yards. Elsewhere, he associates unpleasant odors with various jobs he describes in the packinghouses. Indeed, it might be said that he uses odors as a symbol of the way man has defiled his civilization. A related symbol is the black smoke that issues constantly from the chimneys of the packinghouses. The meaning of these symbols very likely has a more specifically political context for Sinclair. As a Socialist, he would see society as wrongly ordered. Industrialization is not an evil; the evil lies in how it affects men. Industrial progress should benefit men, not degrade or enslave them.

Sinclair's overt use of the hog as a symbol is less effective than his use of either odors or smoke. It is difficult not to smile at his "hog-squeal of the universe," his "heaven for hogs," and his "god of hogs." He obviously means to symbolize the human condition as he finds it; but the hog is not a very apt choice, to say the least.

All of these symbols are related to the overriding symbol in the novel, the jungle. Modern man is like an animal in the jungle: every beast is the prey of some other, and each must look to its own security. Or, to put it in terms of Sinclair's emerging theme, the workingman is the prey of the owner. He lives in a setting hostile to himself, and his chance of survival is slight. Later in the novel, of course, Sinclair broadens his theme to include a way out: collective action.

Two devices of narrative are used in this section: flashback and foreshadowing. The flashback begins in this section and continues through the next (Chapters 4-6). It is appropriate that the novel should start with the wedding feast and only then drop back in time to trace the history of the immigrants' leaving the old world and entering the new. However, Sinclair does not use the device anywhere else in the book.

In a sense, every event foreshadows every other in a novel. If it does not, the author has not structured his plot skillfully. But conspicuous examples can be cited to show how foreshadowing works. The ease with which Jurgis gets his first job is ominous to the thoughtful reader. He is hired because of his obvious size and strength: if he loses these marketable attributes, he will have a hard time getting work in the yards. Another: Jurgis sees the beef-killing operation at Durham's as a marvel of ingenuity. Once down among the workers, he may view it quite differently.

Since above all else Sinclair has a message to convey, he does not hesitate to document his story at times as if he were writing a textbook in economics. Statistics about the operation of the packing industry are quoted, though he attributes them to Jokubas's reading. At one point later in the novel, he even quotes government regulations in a footnote. In addition, he uses what is sometimes called a process description to show what the meat packing operation is like (hog and beef killing), a procedure a little unusual for a novel, though to be found in *Moby Dick* and elsewhere. That he is disguising fact as fiction is evident on occasions such as this and caused a shocked response among readers when the novel first appeared.

CHAPTERS 4-6

Summary

The flashback continuing, Jurgis reports for work at Brown's; and though he quickly learns what it is like to labor on the killing beds he is delighted to be earning money. Both Jonas and Marija are promised work. Jurgis has already decided neither Elzbieta and Ona nor the children should work. Only Dede Antanas does not have a job, and the chances for a man of his age are not very good.

This apparent good fortune causes the family to think about getting a home. Jurgis has picked up a handbill advertising homes for sale. They have already decided they cannot stay where they are and it would be uneconomical to pay rent on an apartment indefinitely. The houses advertised can be bought for a down payment which, together, they can manage, though it will take most of the money they have left. They arrange to visit one of the houses on a Sunday, and though it is not all they expect it to be the agent manages to impress them with its advantages. Later, among themselves, they debate the purchase endlessly, and Jurgis finally has to make the decision to buy.

The actual purchase of the house is an awesome affair to these peasants. Unable to go himself because of his job, Jurgis entrusts Elzbieta and the women with the responsibility, Jokubas Szedvilas going along to assist. In spite of a question about the language of the deed raised by Jokubas, which causes a lawyer to be summoned, Elzbieta goes through with the sale. They are full of apprehension about what they have done and fearful of what Jurgis will say. He is angry about what has happened and immediately goes to a lawyer himself, only to be told as they were that the references to rental in the deed are a matter of form.

Once bought, the house must be furnished. Since they have almost no money left, they must buy furniture on the installment plan. They move in right away, and though there are more people than the house was intended to accommodate they are too grateful to be uncomfortable.

Jurgis's job takes all his energy and strength, but he enjoys it. However, he is shocked to discover that most of the men hate their work and think it is "rotten as hell." He has his first encounter with the union; and though it is attempting to change many working practices, he is unsympathetic, partly because he trusts only in his own strength, partly because unions require dues.

Jurgis begins to learn about corruption in the plants when old Antanas is offered a job at the cost of one-third of his wages. Tamoszius (the fiddler at the wedding) explains that this is a common practice, that every level of employee grafts off the one below, except the workers like themselves who have no one lesser than they. Jurgis finally gives in and lets his father take the job. No sooner does the old man go to work than he begins to startle them all with accounts of unclean practices in the handling of meat.

But Jurgis learns even more. Marija has gotten her job at the expense of a woman who has worked at the same job for years. Marija is the picture of strength; the other woman is sickly. And Jonas replaces a man who was horribly injured by the heavy truck which it is now his job to push. Jurgis himself witnesses the butchering of injured, diseased, or dead cattle that are unfit to eat.

Though Jurgis and Ona have waited a long time to get married, the older people will not allow them to do so without a proper wedding feast, and this is a greater expense than the family can manage now, even though the guests will be expected to contribute enough money to repay them. Ona is thinking of going to work to help raise the money, but a problem with the house sidetracks her plans.

From an old widow in another Lithuanian family in the neighborhood, they learn their house is fifteen years old and the selling price three times the cost of building it. She tells them the company that built it is in business to cheat poor people. Most people default in paying for their homes, and the company sells them over and over. Though she and her son have bought their house, Jurgis and his family are the fifth family to try to buy their house. Each family was a different nationality, reflecting the changes in the labor force in the yards, changes manipulated by the packers to force wages lower and lower.

The first family was German; they had more than half paid for the house, but the father was killed in an accident at work. The next was Irish; the father had been involved in politics. He drank too much and eventually lost his political power. In the next family, which was Bohemian, a child had died of tuberculosis too. The mother of the succeeding family died of the same illness, and the father was killed at work. The house is definitely unlucky, the widow thinks.

The blow comes when the old woman mentions paying interest on the mortgage. The deed is brought out, and they discover she is right. It is yet another expense they have not reckoned on. The result is that Jurgis vows to work harder and Ona and Stanislovas, one of Elzbieta's children, must go to work. Ona gets a job at Brown's, but only after paying the forelady ten dollars. Stanislovas, with a certificate from the priest that he is sixteen (a misrepresentation commonly practiced in Packingtown), gets a job tending a lard machine.

With the child's wages covering the interest payments, the family is about where it was; and again Jurgis and Ona begin to plan how they can hasten their wedding day.

Commentary

The episodes having to do with the house are important at the level of both plot and symbolism. In addition to the fact that a place to live is a concern of any family, the house bodes ill for the future of Jurgis and the others even as they acquire it. It takes virtually all their money to get it, and it will take almost all to keep it. That they cannot possibly succeed is foreshadowed clearly for everyone but them. For example, Ona: the house Ona really wants is the one on the handbill; any actual house will fall short of her expectations. So, of course, the house they buy really is second best. But like the others, she sacrifices to get it and keep it.

As a symbol, it represents a place in the world, something of their own. As peasants, they hesitate a long time to let go of their money for a down payment. However, they feel renting is wasteful because it does not produce anything. As peasants, they also feel that a home of their own is a necessity. Since they are no longer in a country whose values and social climate they understand, they do not realize they have no place in this society and are only part of something called a labor force. As Sinclair makes clear, they have about as much of a place as the animals in the pens: they are to be used.

One other feature of plot may be pointed out. Here, as elsewhere, Sinclair makes use of summary narrative. This is the technique of summarizing what happens rather than dramatizing it with scenes and dialogue. For example, all of the events in Chapter 5 are handled in this way. There are a number of places in which Sinclair might have dramatized an event, but he chooses not to do so. Summary narrative gives less immediacy to a plot, puts the reader at a greater remove. There is less chance for him to identify with either characters or actions. It has the advantage of allowing an author to move rapidly through many events; but used as often as Sinclair employs it, it becomes a defect in the novel. The reader loses interest when he is so often told what is happening rather than being shown.

As in the previous section, and throughout the novel, Sinclair documents the circumstances of his characters' lives in contemporary terms. The reader is told exactly how much each member of the family is earning and what the total family income is as well as the terms of the mortgage on the house. Though not

36

required for the sake of verisimilitude in the novel, such details add to the picture illustrating Sinclair's theme. That workers in the yards can barely eke out an existence is made clear by the almost unbelievable five cents an hour the boy is paid as well as the 17½ cents an hour Jurgis earns.

CHAPTERS 7-9

Summary

The flashback completed, the family tries to recover from the debt left from the wedding as well as the fact that all must return to work the following morning. Jurgis feels more protective than ever towards Ona because he has by now learned that life is "a war of each against all." Yet he is unable to protect her against the weather: not understanding how to get a transfer on the street car, she walks to work in the rain and suffers from working in the cold cellar. There are many things Jurgis has little chance to protect his family from: no sewer to the house; formaldehyde in the milk; shoddy clothing and bedding that offers no warmth.

Nor can he protect his father from the cold cellar he works in or the chemicals soaking through his boots. Suffering from tuberculosis, Antanas finally collapses and soon dies. The family cannot even honor him with a proper funeral; the expense is too great.

The coming of winter brings special hardships to the workers in the yards. Those unfit in any way will be struck down by the hard conditions and quickly replaced from among the thousands of jobless waiting every morning at the gates of the packinghouses. Just getting to work through the cold and snow is a daily struggle. Going to work becomes a nightmare for Stanislovas after seeing another boy's ears broken off when someone rubs them in an attempt to relieve their frozen condition. Even at work, few places are heated, and conditions in the killing beds are especially dangerous. There is no place for the workers to eat, except in one of the innumerable saloons surrounding the yards. And this entails buying at least one drink, if not more, to take advantage of the free lunch. Drinking as an escape from working conditions is common, but Jurgis's respect for Ona saves him from this problem. At home there is not sufficient warmth either. The one small stove the family can afford does not even warm the kitchen; at night they cannot afford to burn any coal at all.

The bitter winter is lightened somewhat by the love that develops between Marija and Tamoszius, an oddly matched couple. He becomes a regular visitor to the house on Sunday afternoons and often takes Marija with him to the parties at which he plays. All the family looks forward to the stories she tells of her travels. Finally, Tamoszius proposes marriage, and they plan for the future. Marija's confidence in herself is shattered when the canning factory where she works is closed down and she is laid off, with little prospect of its reopening very soon.

Jurgis is affected by the end of the holiday rush too: in his case, it means shorter hours and less pay. Normally, though the men must be on the killing beds at seven o'clock, it may be several hours before the cattle start through. Now, for many reasons, including delay in shipments because of bad weather, it may be late in the afternoon before they can work. Cattle must be killed the day they are bought, no matter how late it is. To make matters worse, no man is ever paid for part of an hour's work.

This time when Jurgis is approached to join the union, he is quite willing and also sees to it that all the working members of the family join too. Their membership in the union, however, does not prevent Marija's being laid off; and she makes a passionate speech about it at the first meeting she attends, though few understand her. Jurgis faithfully attends meetings and becomes a zealous convert to unionism, impatient to persuade others.

Jurgis's interests widen as the result of joining the union. He begins to study English so that he can follow what goes on in meetings better. He also begins to learn something of politics.

Though he does not completely understand what is happening, he becomes a citizen at the suggestion of a fellow employee; later he is shown how to vote and is paid $2 to mark his ballot as directed. Jurgis's education in American democracy is a crude but realistic one: "The officials who ruled it, and got all the graft, had to be elected first; and so there were two rival sets of grafters, known as political parties, and the one got the office which bought the most votes."

The political power in the stockyards area is the Democratic boss, Mike Scully. Jurgis hears much of him. It is Scully's dump and brickyard he and Ona saw on their first day in Packingtown. He is a man of great influence, able to manipulate the city government to benefit his own business interests and apparently in control of all the graft in the area. His organization is the "War-Whoop League," whose members are used chiefly to buy votes in elections and keep the channels of graft open. One of the "Indians" was Jurgis's guide in gaining citizenship. It is to Scully the packers are said to come when they need concessions from the city.

The men tell Jurgis a great deal about what the packers have gotten away with. He hears about "Bubbly Creek," that arm of the Chicago River which is an open sewer, and about the way they steal water from the city. He discovers that government inspection is a fraud and that even this sham is not required for meat sold in the city or state. And the canned meat at Durham's —he is told of the chemical processes by which almost any kind of scrap can be turned into potted chicken or deviled ham. The canning of horsemeat has only recently been stopped.

Now that he is no longer an observer but a worker, Jurgis notices the occupational diseases of his fellow employees. All those who use knives have little left of the thumb; those who work in the chilling rooms have rheumatism; the wool pluckers lose fingers from the acid used to loosen the wool on the sheep; and so on.

Commentary

In the commentary on the previous section (Chapters 4-6), Sinclair's use of summary narrative is discussed. It will be noticed that the present section is developed in this way, entirely without a dramatic scene. Any number of incidents might have been dramatized: for instance, Tamoszius's proposal of marriage or Marija's speech at the union meeting. The ingredients for drama are present, but Sinclair's purpose in the novel or perhaps his abilities as a fiction writer dictate a different use of these ingredients. In addition to the disadvantages already mentioned, the extensive use of summary narrative undermines the reality of the characters, making them seem like illustrative props rather than willful human beings.

Sinclair depicts Jurgis's idea of Ona as a simple one: "she was so sensitive—she was not fitted for such a life as this"; and her husband sees mainly her "simple goodness." His reaction to her is protective, as he begins to see that life is a perpetual war in which the weak do not survive. He is incapable of realizing that what is most characteristic of her is that which he is least capable of protecting, her goodness. It seems likely that he will be unable even to protect her life. But this goodness he sees in her is the standard by which he judges himself and finds he is not good enough for her. As in other matters, here Jurgis is shown to have a narrow range of understanding and awareness. He is truly a peasant.

If Ona has few of the characteristics needed to survive in the hostile world Sinclair pictures, Marija is the opposite. She has physical strength like Jurgis, but more than that she has resourcefulness. This makes the relationship between her and Tamoszius even more comic. Like Jurgis and his muscles, this little man is distinguished in only one way: by his music. Perhaps it is because he is not strong in body but powerful in his ability to communicate with music that Marija is taken by him. He makes love to her with his violin, but it is difficult to imagine them in any domestic scene as man and wife. Yet they would be no more oddly matched than Jurgis and Ona.

It may well be that the simple characters Sinclair uses accurately reflect the people and the times of his story. It is true that he shows them all from the outside, that they are defined almost exclusively by what they do. But certainly it is Sinclair's purpose to show the life of the workingman, especially the immigrant. The question may be raised as to whether he has oversimplified his human beings in order to demonstrate better the message he conveys. If he has, it is no more than any other propagandist does. His assumptions about human nature surely are that men are shaped by the society in which they live and that, given a different society, men will develop to whatever degree their capacities allow. Whether Jurgis's conversion to Socialism in the last part of the novel is any kind of demonstration of the truth of the second assumption is an open question.

Once again, Sinclair in this section documents the setting and the problems he depicts. What he says of politics in Chicago was not news when the book was published; other muckrakers had exposed political corruption. Some of what he says about practices in the packinghouses was also public information. But to this he adds the force of his own observations. This kind of documentation—for example; the occupational diseases of the workers—is more effective than a footnote quoting government regulations.

The overall metaphor of the jungle is supported throughout the novel by the image of life as a war. Though not original, it is true to the conditions Sinclair depicts. He applies it to the way Jurgis learns to look at life around him and implies that all men in these conditions are bound to see things in the same way. More striking, perhaps, is the description Sinclair uses to indicate the effect of winter on the workers of Packingtown. "Now the dreadful winter was come upon them. In the forests, all summer long, the branches of the trees do battle for light, and some of them lose and die; and then come the raging blasts, and the storms of snow and hail, and strew the ground with these weaker branches. Just so it was in Packingtown; the whole district braced itself for the struggle that was an agony, and those whose time was come died off in hordes." It is curious that here Sinclair, who is not distinguished by his use of language, sounds almost stately and Biblical. Certainly the image is an apt one, and also relates to the idea of the jungle.

CHAPTERS 10-12

Summary

By spring, with Jurgis's earnings still reduced and the canning factory where Marija worked still not reopened, the family is struggling just to survive. And the house brings them one problem after another: in addition to repairs, they must pay for insurance, taxes, and water taxes as well as sidewalks if the city decides to lay them.

Summer brings little relief. After the spring rains comes the heat; the killing beds at Durham's are stifling and Packingtown is covered with flies. After going back to work when the canning factory opens again, Marija loses her job. She thinks it is because of her activities in the union. An occasion has arisen when she is cheated out of her pay for some of the cans she paints and persists in taking the matter to the superintendent.

With Ona pregnant, it is a bad time for Marija to lose her job. After weeks of looking, she is finally hired as a beef trimmer, a job normally filled by a man. Her job is to trim the meat of diseased animals in a canning factory. Since the family needs her wages, she must once again postpone marrying Tamoszius. As dissatisfied as Marija, Ona will not protest for fear of losing her job. She discovers her forelady operates a brothel downtown, and is living there with a man who is boss of the loading gang. He frequently fires the decent girls to give jobs to her prostitutes.

Ona's baby is born, with the assistance of the male doctor Jurgis insists on having instead of a midwife. Because of his long hours, however, Jurgis sees little of his son, Antanas, and Ona must go back to work at Brown's only a week after the child is born. Not strong to begin with, Ona will suffer the same ailments as most of the women who work in the plants and will never be in good health again.

Jurgis does make more money in the summer but not as much as in the previous one. This is because of several practices, such as hiring more new men than are needed; constantly speeding up the pace of work; and constantly reducing wages. Jurgis also learns that the packers act in concert on these and other matters, that there is something called the Beef Trust.

Marija worries little about these matters and, confident of herself, opens a savings account at a bank. But her naive fears about what might happen to her money are realized when there is a run on the bank. She misses work and stands in line with thousands of other people for almost two days before she can get into the bank and get her money. Once she has it in her hands, she wants to deposit it again but is not allowed to do so. As it turns out, the run resulted from an incident having no connection with the bank.

When winter comes, the family does not feel ready for it; and Jurgis worries especially about Ona. The first bad storm lasts four days, and it takes all Jurgis's strength to get himself, Ona, and Stanislovas back and forth to work. Jurgis is proud of his mastery of the elements, but he is undone soon after from an unexpected event. During one of those occasions when a steer breaks loose on the killing beds and there is confusion among the crew, Jurgis sprains his ankle. He ignores it until the next day and then is in too much pain to continue working.

The impact on the family is immediate. They have just barely been getting by, and the loss of one income is critical. Besides that, those still working face the slack season. Jurgis too knows the plight they are in, and for the first time he fears that life may defeat him. Elzbieta looks after him, and the only way she can calm him is to interest him in his baby son.

After three weeks in bed, Jurgis goes to work, only to discover he cannot stand the pain. The doctor who is finally called discovers that Jurgis has a pulled tendon; it will be another two months before he can work. Meanwhile, another storm hits and Ona and Stanislovas are unable to get to work. In the struggle to do so, the boy freezes his fingers and ends up having the joints of several fingers permanently disabled. Thereafter, Jurgis must beat him to get him to go to work.

One consequence of their struggle to live is that Jonas leaves in the early spring. Though he has worked regularly and contributed his wages to the family, he has gotten little of the simple comforts he desires. With Jonas gone, they decide that Elzbieta's two younger sons must leave school and go to work. The boys are sent downtown to learn to sell newspapers. With the family borrowing from both Marija and Tamoszius, they can see no other course to take.

Ona has suffered a good deal all this time, from the weather and from the fact that she has so little support from Jurgis. She wonders at times if he still loves her, but he is so burdened with worries that he does not respond to her needs.

Finally, in the spring Jurgis is able to go to work again. Since his job at Brown's is gone, he joins the ranks of job seekers. When he tries all the plants as well as asking his fellow union members for help, he begins to realize the position he is in. No longer is he vigorous and strong, standing out from the crowd of men waiting at the gates of the plants. Now he is a "damaged article." Even his accident, for which the company refuses liability, gives him no claim on a job. It is up to the boss as to whether a man is taken back. In a case where the company is liable, it has deceptive ways of dealing with a man.

Commentary

As has been said earlier, the character of Jurgis is drawn on simple lines. As a transplanted peasant, he is shown to be interested only in what concerns him directly; the realm of ideas is closed to him, for the most part, and he does not easily relate events to each other in order to see their meaning. However, in this section, when he is unable to work, he has time to reflect at least on his own experience. "It might be true, then, after all, what others had told him about life, that the best powers of a man might not be equal to it!" This is a very novel idea to him and a very frightening one. It is in marked contrast to his resolution to work harder as a solution to all problems.

But he manages to go even a step beyond this understanding. His inactivity as the result of his injury is followed by a fruitless search for work. He begins to understand why this is so. "In the beginning he had been fresh and strong, and he had gotten a job the first day; but now he was secondhand, a damaged article, so to speak, and they did not want him." And he realizes that other men have undergone the same experience. Indeed, he suspects that the packers do this on purpose. Though he may be unable to understand the Beef Trust as representing a defect in the structure of society, he does now realize the effects of it on the worker. He still does not understand what the union means as a force in society or even what the workers can do in any kind of organization.

On the level of plot, Jurgis's injury is a clear foreshadowing of what will happen to him. As pointed out earlier, the very qualities that cause him to be hired so easily may, in turn, be the cause of his undoing. Once he is no longer "fresh and strong," he has little chance to survive in the jungle of Packingtown. At this point, he is frightened by the prospect of failure; but he is unable, like the reader, to see his future destiny.

In this critical time, Jurgis is concerned primarily for himself. Ona is quite right, in a sense; he does not love her as he did simply because too many shattering experiences are happening to him for him to be able to extend his sympathy and understanding to her. This may be a defect in his character, but it is a human one. Certainly Ona is in need of both understanding and help. As Sinclair points out, she falls victim to the "womb trouble" all the women suffer from and is made to pay a high price for events over which she has no control, for example, having to work and bearing Jurgis's child. And she has to endure even more for the sake of helping the family survive. It offends her to work with the keeper and the inhabitants of a brothel, but she is afraid that if Jurgis finds out he will insist she quit the job even though the family will suffer. And as the novel will reveal later she has to put up with even more than this.

If Jurgis's strength is not sufficient for survival in this hostile world they are trying to live in, neither is Ona's goodness. Certainly her ailments are a clear foreshadowing of the fact that she will not survive. In a way, her virtue undoes her even as Jurgis's strength is the cause of his undoing. Were she not so determined to suffer in silence, to endure whatever indignities come to her as the result of her job, what happens to her might be different. Of course, only the reader sees this; only the objective observer says about someone else, never himself, that this life could be otherwise.

Sinclair's use of time in his plot, as illustrated in this section, is a little awkward. The seasonal changes are important to the story because they bring new obstacles and problems for the characters to face. The problems, however, are the important thing to show. The seasons come and go abruptly and unnaturally. Time does not flow smoothly, in short, and the reader is too aware of the author's turning to a new season in order to put the characters through their paces once more. Perhaps this awkwardness comes from Sinclair's impatience with the form of the novel in his desire to illustrate his theme.

This theme is driven home a number of times in this section. In a world hostile to them, all the characters learn the hard lesson of hanging on to a job once they have it. Marija must learn it; Ona puts up with much because she fears to learn the lesson the hard way. They are at the mercy of those who hire, as Jurgis sees after he recovers from his accident. Sinclair points out one of the consequences of this absolute dependence of worker on boss: "under such circumstances immorality was exactly as inevitable, and as prevalent, as it was under the system of chattel slavery." And behind this system of new chattel slavery stands the Beef Trust, that combination of packers which, in Sinclair's opinion, holds more power than any government. That Jurgis with all his strength has little chance against this powerful force is a foregone conclusion, Or, at least, so Sinclair demonstrates through most of the novel.

46

Though Sinclair's imagery is rather conventional, sometimes even a conventional image can be effective if apt. Such is the case with the image of Jurgis as a "monarch of the forest." It is used to describe Jurgis after he has successfully battled the winter's first bad storm and before he slips and twists a tendon. "When it was over, the soul of Jurgis was a song, for he had met the enemy and conquered, and felt himself the master of his fate. So it might be with some monarch of the forest that has vanquished his foes in fair fight, and then falls into some cowardly trap in the nighttime." This simile is appropriate to the tall, powerful Jurgis. And it fits in well with the idea of the jungle which is used to symbolize Packingtown and all such places like it.

CHAPTERS 13-15

Summary

During Jurgis's search for work, another crisis occurs in the family. One of Elzbieta's two crippled sons dies. Jurgis insists that there is no money for a funeral, and Elzbieta is even more hysterical in her grief. A funeral is held, however, with the help of Marija and the neighbors, from whom the mother begs money.

All that Jurgis is able to think about now is that he may be forced to take a job in the fertilizer plant at Durham's. It has a reputation among the men of being the last resort. In the basement, waste products like blood and bone are made into saleable products, but the smells there make working conditions almost intolerable. On the first floor, however, conditions are even worse. Here, the tankage is ground to a powder and made into fertilizer. The combination of smell and dust from the powder make it a place that the men avoid if possible.

Though Jurgis has applied for a job here, he hopes he will not be needed. When he is offered a job on a hot June day, he takes it because he must and vows to stick it out. Within minutes after going to work shoveling fertilizer into carts when it comes from the grinding mill, he is covered with dust and is suffering from headaches and dizziness. He is a pariah on the street car, and his presence at home is enough to make all the family ill. But he does continue to work.

Jurgis and the family are especially troubled by the life Elzbieta's sons are leading downtown as they sell newspapers. They are exposed to all the vices of the city, and they get out of the habit of coming home every night. Jurgis decides they will return to school in the fall even though this means Elzbieta must go to work and Kotrina, only thirteen, must take care of her surviving crippled brother.

Elzbieta's job is tending a sausage machine. In a damp basement, she places a casing over a nozzle on the stuffing machine and fills it with sausage meat, which is supplied from large mixing bowls on the other side of the room. Other women tie the filled casings into links and strings.

With the family working in a variety of jobs in the packinghouses, they learn a great deal about the various "Packingtown swindles." Hams are pickled in a matter of seconds, and those that are slightly spoiled are treated in various ways and sold. The completely spoiled hams go into sausage meat, along with other meat scraps and garbage of all sorts.

Jurgis, Ona, Elzbieta—all are beginning to sense defeat in their struggle for something more than a bare existence. They came to America for a better life, and though they are usually too tired to remember this dream they have not forgotten it completely. For Jurgis, this sense of defeat expresses itself in a struggle with liquor. With a job which keeps him feeling ill all the time, drinking seems to be a way of gaining some moments of peace. Most of the men who work at the fertilizer plant try to use liquor this way, but for Jurgis it is at first a great extravagance. Sometimes being with Ona is a way to keep out of saloons; at other times, he wishes she would drink with him.

It is not very pleasant at home for Jurgis right now. Antanas has the measles, and Ona is more and more often hysterical. He cannot understand why she is this way since she has never been so before. And she is unable to explain. Elzbieta tells Jurgis it is because Ona is pregnant again that she acts as she does. He does not believe this and fears something mysterious is going on that he is not told about.

Soon winter is upon them, and again the holiday rush. They all work long hours and can hardly keep track of the passing days and nights. Shortly before Thanksgiving, after a snowstorm, Ona fails to return home after work. Elzbieta awakens Jurgis in the morning with this news, and he immediately sets off to search for her. Unable to get news of her, he finally waits at the plant where she works. When she does come, late for work, she tells him she tried to get home, couldn't make it, and stayed with a friend. Jurgis feels she is more upset than the occasion demands but thinks no more of it.

Shortly before Christmas, again Ona does not come home. Awakend at midnight with the news, Jurgis assumes she has stayed with the friend again and goes back to sleep. But in the morning he goes to the friend's house, to discover she is not there. Nor, he learns, was she ever there before. After waiting outside the plant where Ona works, he goes inside and inquires of her fellow employees, who seem to know something they won't tell him. He waits outside until mid-afternoon and then sets out for home. By chance he sees Ona on a street car and follows her home.

Pushing aside Elzbieta, who tells him Ona has been home all day, Jurgis confronts his wife in their bedroom and demands to know where she has been. He will not be put off by the story she tells, and when he says he has seen her get off the street car from downtown she collapses on the floor. She breaks into hysterical crying, which finally brings Elzbieta into the room. Almost throwing her out, Jurgis, though resolute, is dismayed by Ona's condition; he shouts at her to stop. When she does, she tries to get him to forget what she as yet has not told him. But in answer to his demands, she does tell him she has been to the house of her forelady. It takes him awhile to realize what this means.

He forces from her the fact that it is Connor, the boss of the loading gang near the department where she works, who has taken her downtown. Jurgis makes her tell him the history of their relationship, and Ona reveals that Connor has used threats to get them all fired in order to make her go with him. Ona has not known how to evade him. She tells him that Connor was tired of her anyway, that Jurgis need not have known about it.

Leaving her behind, Jurgis rushes out of the room, out of the house, and into the streets. He runs until he is exhausted and then takes a street car the rest of the way to the plant. He finds Connor and jumps him before the man can get away. He knocks the Irishman down and tries to strangle him. The abrupt attack throws the place into confusion, and it takes many men some time to pull Jurgis off Connor and subdue him. Jurgis is taken to the company police station to await a patrol wagon.

Commentary

One of the most noteworthy aspects of this section is Sinclair's use of a long dramatic scene between Ona and Jurgis. Part of the reason why it is worth noting is that there are so few in the novel. His usual technique is summary narrative. However, the plot calls for a confrontation between husband and wife, for several reasons. The demands on Jurgis have been so great that his feelings for Ona have been deadened. She has been shown to wonder if Jurgis still loves her and is unable to get him to respond satisfactorily. On the other side, her behavior has become unaccountable to Jurgis; he is said to believe that he is not being told things he ought to know. He can't understand her hysterical weeping as well as her overreactions on some occasions. This confrontation might have been handled in summary, but Sinclair chose to dramatize it.

The choice may not have been a happy one judged on the basis of effect. The scene has much of the air of melodrama, though certainly Sinclair did not intend it to be so. Jurgis stands over Ona, demanding to know the truth, even almost strangling her at one point in his zeal to get this "truth." Ona is prostrate before him, hysterical, groveling, nearly inarticulate. Certain situations seem invariably to produce this stereotyped (or archetypal, depending on the point of view) behavior; adultery revealed is one of them. However, the question in a novel is not whether it is a recording of actual behavior but whether it artfully seems to be. Sinclair's ability to make the scene between Ona and Jurgis believable is in question.

Before he walks into the bedroom to confront Ona, Jurgis is already deeply suspicious. He has discovered Ona's deception about staying with a friend, he has been aware that her fellow employees know something about her that he doesn't, he has seen her get off the street car from downtown, and he has built up a backlog of doubt because of her increasingly hysterical behavior. His "Where have you been?" addressed to her, without even a greeting, is almost an anti-climax. Yet, like all human beings, he must know the "truth." In this matter of truth, it turns out that perhaps Ona is wiser than her husband. If she is inarticulate and hesitant in answering him, it may be that she has learned that truth is deceptive and many-sided. And what truth does Jurgis eventually learn? He learns that Ona has been unable to control the circumstances which determine her life. Her going with Connor to the brothel is no more a choice on her part than Jurgis's working in the fertilizer plant is his decision. But to Jurgis, Ona's unfaithfulness is a deep injury. His truth is the truth of striking back, of making someone accountable. Her truth is the cry for recognition from another human being: "Believe me!" Ona is able to understand his truth; Jurgis is unable to understand hers.

In short, the essential point of confrontation between husband and wife is believable. The behavior attributed to them is less so. When Jurgis reveals he has seen Ona get off the street car from downtown, she goes "all to pieces." "For half a second she stood, reeling and swaying, staring at him with horror in her eyes; then, with a cry of anguish, she tottered forward, stretching out her arms to him." Jurgis keeps demanding an explanation, but Ona does not respond. "Yet she did not hear him — she was still in the grip of the fiend. Jurgis could see her outstretched hands, shaking and twitching, roaming here and there over the bed at will, like living things; he could see convulsive shudderings start in her body and run through her limbs. . . . her voice would begin to rise into screams, louder and louder until it broke in wild, horrible peals of laughter." There is much more of such behavior described.

It is not that a woman like Ona might not act this way; it is that her actions are excessive in relation to the norm of behavior already established in the novel. In addition, Ona's previous emotional outbursts have never been presented dramatically, only in summary. A reader can be led to believe almost anything if he is prepared for it. Sinclair's description might be believable in, for example, a Gothic novel. This same analysis holds true for the character of Jurgis. It takes him a moment to understand where she has been, once she has managed to tell him. "And he reeled and staggered back with a scream. He caught himself against the wall, and put his hands to his forehead, staring about him, and whispering, 'Jesus! Jesus!'" Then, Jurgis puts his hands around her throat and exerts more pressure than he realizes. "He tightened his grip, in his frenzy, and only when he saw her eyes closing did he realize that he was choking her. Then he relaxed his fingers, and crouched, waiting, until she opened her lids again. His breath beat hot into her face."

In this section, a great deal of evidence is present to show that the lives of the principal characters are turning for the worse. Jurgis has reached the last resort in employment for the men in Packingtown, the fertilizer plant. He has accepted· continual headaches and other pains as the condition of his life. Ona has been forced to make love to Connor in a brothel, and her ill health is now matched by her disturbed emotional state. And this occurs while she is pregnant with her second child. Jurgis is finally reduced to an animal in his attack on Connor, literally becoming an animal as he tears flesh from the man's cheek with his teeth. What is foreshadowed in earlier sections is now coming true. Jurgis and Ona begin to see that defeat is an imminent reality.

Thematically, Jurgis's act is a measure of the conditions causing this defeat. The family did not come to a new country to be dehumanized. "They had dreamed of freedom; of a chance to look about them and learn something; to be decent and clean, to see their child grow up to be strong." They have not lost sight of this dream, but when they look around them they see so little chance of ever realizing it. "They were beaten; they had lost the game, they were swept aside." It is this sense of defeat which, as she tries to explain to Jurgis, made Ona know that resisting Connor was futile. It is frustration in defeat which drives Jurgis to try to strangle Connor. That it is Connor in both cases is, of course, significant. He is not the cause of their defeat, only an indication of why it occurs. He is a boss, next up on a hierarchy from which they are excluded. It is a hierarchy of power built on fear. Most expendable are those at the bottom like Jurgis and Ona.

Two lapses in technique in this section are, if nothing else, at least awkward. In the midst of a description of additional spoiled-meat practices typical of the packinghouses, Sinclair says, "This is no fairy story and no joke." This addressing the reader directly undermines a verisimilitude which at best is constantly veering away from fiction into fact. A contemporary novelist might very well use such a device to deliberately provoke the reader into disbelief; in Sinclair's novel, it is simply clumsiness. So also with the author's withholding knowledge of Ona's trips to the brothel as if Jurgis were the point of view from which the story is told. Of course, he is not; the point of view is that of the omniscient author. It would have been awkward to reveal this knowledge sooner than Sinclair does; it is awkward as well to hold off as long as he does. A limited point of view has many advantages; but in 1905 this technique was not yet widely used.

Sinclair continues to document the unsanitary practices he observed in the packinghouses. The passage on hams and sausage in this section—one of those that so aroused contemporary readers of the novel—is included in the story ostensibly because members of the family are working at a variety of jobs in Packingtown. This is a very thin pretext, but it is sufficient to serve the purposes of propaganda. Jurgis's struggle with liquor is an interesting instance of documentation. It is true that drinking was widespread among the unskilled workers for the reasons Sinclair gives. The nature of working conditions in the yards and the attraction of the saloon as a social institution are two of these. In addition, Sinclair was a militant teetotaler, in part because of his father. Throughout the novel, he insists that "drink" is a major vice. Yet he is sympathetic with the workingman who turns to liquor for relief; after all, it is society which is really at fault.

CHAPTERS 16-17

Summary

Jurgis is taken to a police station, booked on a charge of assault and battery, and jailed. He does not resist, knowing what the police would do to him if he did. Once his satisfaction at having gotten revenge on Connor has passed, Jurgis is tormented by what has happened to Ona. It is impossible for him to change the past, but it is equally impossible for him to live with it. The presence of neither the other prisoners nor the homeless who come in after midnight can distract his thoughts. He imagines in vivid detail what will happen to the family and is certain they will lose the house for which they all have struggled so hard.

In the morning he is taken before a magistrate, who happens to be the notorious Justice Callahan, a part of the political machine, like Scully, which controls Packingtown. When the company lawyer appearing for Connor asks for and is granted a postponement and Jurgis is unable to post bond, he is taken to the county jail to await trial. He is made to bathe and is housed in a small cell by himself. Unable to sleep and driven by his thoughts, he is startled by the chimes which begin at midnight; it is Christmas Eve. Memories of Christmas in Lithuania come to him, as well as recollections of the frugal celebrations the family has managed in this new country. But the bells are not ringing for him. It is a mockery that enrages him. His family may be starving and homeless; but, though locked up, he is being fed and housed. He curses a society which permits such insanity and injustice. It is the "beginning of his rebellion."

In the morning another prisoner is put in the cell with Jurgis, and he meets Jack Duane. The fact that Duane acts like a gentleman but is in jail puzzles Jurgis; however, he is pleased that the young man will talk so freely with him, a mere working man. Duane tells Jurgis much about himself and about what led to his becoming a safecracker. His attitude of perpetual war against society is one that Jurgis is beginning to understand. He also encourages Jurgis to talk about himself. It is Duane who introduces him to many of the other prisoners, and for the first time Jurgis encounters the sick side of society at first hand and is frightened by it. Duane gives Jurgis an address where he can be located, and the latter is taken back to court for trial.

Elzbieta and Kotrina are in the courtroom, in response to the postcard Jurgis had Duane write for him; and so also is Connor. Anger rises in Jurgis again, and he is almost disappointed the man is still alive. Connor's testimony is false, but Justice Callahan obviously is willing to believe whatever he says. Given a chance to speak, Jurgis does not know what he can say. Finally, through a translator, he tries to explain what happened to Ona. The judge pays little attention and sentences Jurgis to thirty days imprisonment. He has little sympathy for Jurgis's pleas in behalf of his family.

Imprisoned in the Bridewell with petty criminals, Jurgis has an unpleasant time of it; unlike his days with Jack Duane. And he is unnerved by a visit from Stanislovas. The boy comes to get money from Jurgis and relates one disaster after another: Marija's hand cut, the house payment unpaid, Stanislovas' job lost, Kotrina on the street selling newspapers. The most disturbing news—unbelievable to Jurgis—is that Ona tried to get her job back and was refused by her forelady and cursed by Connor. Jurgis gives the boy all he has, fourteen cents, and is so shaken by the visit he can hardly stand.

Commentary

The education of Jurgis Rudkus is both broadened and intensified in this section. It is broadened in that he encounters people and experiences he previously had no contact with, in that he begins to see he is not alone in feeling outcast, and in that he becomes aware of alternatives, whether desirable or not, to the way of life he has been leading. His education is intensified in the sense that he feels personally responsible as well as anguished about the consequences of his own acts, even as, at the same time, he recognizes society as unjust.

Until he is in jail, Jurgis has been so immersed in his own problems and his own grievances that he has scarcely even recognized Ona's struggles. Indeed, his reaction to Ona's forced confession of adultery was clearly one of concern for himself, not his wife. Now, his second thoughts are quite different: "that he had nearly killed the boss would not help Ona—not the horrors that she had borne, nor the memory that would haunt her all her days." He finds there is no way to escape the "tyranny of the past," but it is difficult to accept that past as irrevocable.

And this leads him to his own role in the past. "Ah, if only he could have foreseen it—but then, he would have foreseen it, if he had not been a fool!" What he says is less important than the fact that he says it. After all, for "fool" it is possible to substitute "human being." And even if wisdom is not the result in the future, at least Jurgis has seen himself in relation to another. Hindsight is better than no sight at all.

The certain loss of the house is another painful thought. It is more than just a house to him and the family: "how much he had suffered for this house, how much they had all of them suffered! It was their one hope of respite, as long as they lived; they had put all their money into it—and they were working people, poor people, whose money was their strength, the very substance of them, body and soul, the thing by which they lived and for lack of which they died." It is, of course, a symbol, as was pointed out earlier. It is so much a symbol of their hopes, their claim to status that Jurgis cannot even imagine any other habitation. Turned out of the house, the family will be on the streets, to freeze and starve to death.

The fact that his family will be turned out of the house, while Jurgis is locked up in a warm cell and fed, is the bridge in his thinking which leads him to pronounce "ten thousand curses" on a society which will permit such inhumanity to occur. "There was no justice, there was no right, anywhere in it—it was only force, it was tyranny, the will and the power, reckless and unrestrained!" As yet, his response is one of protest; the only action he can think of is revenge, as earlier he has struck down the boss Connor. But he does accuse in more than just individual terms.

Sinclair reinforces his picture of Jurgis's education in order to hammer home his theme. "These midnight hours were fateful ones to Jurgis; in them was the beginning of his rebellion, of his outlawry and his unbelief. He had no wit to trace back the social crime to its far sources—he could not say that it was the thing men have called 'the system' that was crushing him to the earth; that it was the packers, his masters, who had bought up the law of the land, and had dealt out their brutal will to him from the seat of justice." Jurgis will learn that though other alternatives are open within the system it is the system itself which is at fault and must be replaced. But this aspect of his education is yet in the future.

An alternative, of course, is revealed by Jack Duane and the prisoners to whom he introduces Jurgis. Duane's choice is that of "a genial freebooter, living off the enemy." He is at war with society; sometimes he wins a battle and other times he loses. This attitude at first appalls Jurgis, but he is beginning to see why a man might choose such a life. Other men in prison represent the range of criminal acts, other choices open to Jurgis. Sinclair describes them as "the drainage of the great festering ulcer of society." Jurgis too is sickened by what he sees; yet, he is here because he has tried to take a man's life. That they should all be viewed by society in the same way is a realization Jurgis slowly is becoming aware of.

The presence of Duane at this point in the story is an interesting use of a technique of characterization in order to serve the plot. His only purpose is to act as a connector. It is by means of Duane's presence that Jurgis is shown alternatives and a side of life he has been completely unaware of. He would have encountered the prisoners in any case, but his relationship to Duane makes the contact meaningful. Also, later in the book, Duane is used to involve Jurgis in quite a different life from that of working in the packinghouses.

Sinclair repeats his overall symbol of the jungle in describing the men in prison. He speaks of the "wild-beast tangle" into which they are born and of how, in this irrational society, men "fell upon each other like wolves in a pit." It may be that they happen to be in the city of Chicago, but they would have exactly the same life and the same chance no matter where they lived. Sinclair is unrelenting in his picture of the corruption of life in Chicago, but he implies that no other city is better.

CHAPTERS 18-19

Summary

Finally released from the Bridewell after serving extra days in lieu of paying court costs, Jurgis starts for home. He walks extra miles in the winter weather because of being given wrong directions, but he does make it to the center of the city and continues the long walk to Packingtown. All this time he thinks about what has happened to his family.

When he finally reaches his house, he is puzzled by its changed appearance and a strange child who comes out the front door. He demands to know what strangers are doing in his house, only to find out that his fears have been realized. The house is no longer his. From a Lithuanian neighbor he demands to know the whereabouts of his family and is told they are back at the Widow Jukniene's. The fact that what he thought would happen while he was in prison has come about increases his despair. He sees that the family have been victims from the first; now that the system has used them up they have been cast aside.

Jurgis finds the family at the widow's. Almost the first thing he hears is a scream of pain from Ona, but the women will not let him go to her. Marija explains that the baby has come early and they are not able to afford even a midwife, let alone a doctor. Since he was at work when Antanas was born, he is unused to what is happening and is upset by Ona's cries. At the widow's urging, the women give all they have to Jurgis, and he goes to find a midwife with the dollar and a quarter.

The one he applies to is Madame Haupt, a very fat, very dirty-looking woman. Jurgis is impatient, in a hurry to bring help to Ona and put an end to her terrible cries. But the woman is reluctant, having just returned from a case, and questions Jurgis relentlessly about his ability to pay. While he can think only of his need, she wants to bargain for a fee. She does finally agree to come only when Jurgis starts to leave in anger. She complains about the distance she will have to go, is slow in getting ready, and cannot keep up with the pace Jurgis sets. Once at the widow's, Madame Haupt refuses to climb the ladder to the attic where Ona is, and where the family has been living, but is finally persuaded to do so.

Sent out of the house, Jurgis goes to a saloon he has frequented in the past and begs a drink and a meal. He has not eaten since he was released from prison. The proprietor lets him warm up for awhile, but instead of running Jurgis out when the crowd gathers later he lets him sleep on the basement steps. But Jurgis cannot sleep and returns to the widow's before dawn.

He arrives to discover the baby is not born yet. However, Madame Haupt laboriously descends soon after with bad news. The baby has not survived, and Ona is dying. Jurgis cannot believe what she reports and rushes up to the attic. A priest is with Ona, who is emaciated and white. For a moment when Jurgis calls to her, she seems to recognize him, but then she is gone. Fear and despair grip Jurgis, and he cannot control himself. He is unable to accept that fact that she is dead at eighteen. In the morning, he comes downstairs, demands money from Kotrina, who has just come in from several days of selling newspapers, and goes to the nearest saloon to get drunk.

Commentary

The death of Ona is the turning point in the plot of the novel. The book begins with the celebration of the wedding of Ona and Jurgis, and to Jurgis his bride represents all that is good in life. His coming to America in search of freedom and his desire to build a good life for Ona are inextricably bound together. Because of her youth and fragility, Jurgis feels a great need to protect her. Now, however, Ona is dead. He has not found freedom, he and his family are living in squalor, and he has been unable to protect Ona from the shattering events of the last three years. Every step has been a move in the direction opposite to his dreams; and though he is now beginning to understand why his hopes have been blighted, as yet he has not found any other way out. Of course, Jurgis will try other alternatives; and in the end he will discover Socialism as an alternative to the system that has broken him. But on the level of human relationships it will not quite be the same without Ona. The death of his son Antanas in the next section merely reinforces the turning point represented in Ona's death.

Earlier, Sinclair's use of minor characters was discussed. Madame Haupt is another example of this kind of character, though she is developed as less of a stereotype than some. She is believable, certainly, from her first appearance. "She was a Dutch woman, enormously fat—when she walked she rolled like a small boat on the ocean, and the dishes in the cupboard jostled each other. She wore a filthy blue wrapper, and her teeth were black." Her attitude is shaped by her calling of midwife: she is called only because she is needed and usually never soon enough, and everyone tries to cheat her of her fee. Jurgis's impatience is an everyday occurrence to her. Sinclair seems to imply that she is typical of midwives, no more ignorant and dirty than most. No one likes her, but she is an unavoidable necessity. Few in Packingtown can afford a doctor, as Jurgis did at the birth of his first child. The character of Madame Haupt reveals something of the quality of life in the environment in which the story is set. From the point of view of plot, it is appropriate that the event which serves as the turning point should be presided over, in part, by such a one as this midwife.

On the level of setting, it is to be noticed that the family is back at the widow's when Ona's death occurs. This also reinforces the significant change in the plot. They have lost the house which represented so much to all of them. They are not merely back at the widow's; they are forced to live in her attic, which is without heat or a real floor. While in prison, Jurgis imagined his family homeless on the street. The attic is the step just prior to this.

The revelation about society which Jurgis underwent in prison is continued in his reaction to losing the house. He traces the history of their undoing, and now sees that it was inevitable from the start: they have been victims from "the first lying circular" about the house through "all the tricks of the packers" and the "mercilessness of the city" to "this last hideous injustice" of being turned out of their home. "And they could do nothing, they were tied hand and foot—the law was against them, the whole machinery of society was at their oppressors' command!" This is not merely a restatement of Sinclair's theme; it is that theme as it becomes a part of the experience of Jurgis.

CHAPTERS 20-21

Summary

Unable to stay drunk very long on the money he has, Jurgis returns home ashamed of himself. Ona is not yet buried, and Elzbieta is out begging enough money to pay for a mass. In the attic, next to Ona's body he thinks of her: how she was in Lithuania, how she suffered, how he loved her, how she is gone from him forever. Neither Marija nor Elzbieta scold him. But Elzbieta pleads with him to remember his son, to think of what Ona would want him to do. She presses him to promise to look for work, and he cannot do anything but agree.

At Durham's fertilizer mill Jurgis is turned down by his former boss. After a week of looking and hanging about the saloons, he is offered a job at Jones's. But when he returns the next day to go to work, the boss tells him he can't use him. Jurgis then knows he is blacklisted, and the men tell him he will be unable to work in the packinghouses in any city. Since Marija and Elzbieta do not want to leave Packingtown because they expect work in the yards, they decide Jurgis should look downtown, with financial help from the newspaper sales of the children.

For several weeks, along with thousands of others, he looks for work and occasionally earns a little money. A chance meeting with a union acquaintance leads to a job in the harvester works. This very large establishment offers much better working conditions than the packinghouses. However, the jobs are all specialized as in the yards; and many are piece work. Jurgis is fascinated by the machines which mass produce parts for the harvesters and observes the repetitious work done by the men who tend them. Though he must walk many miles to work, his morale is so improved that he begins to plan for the future. Maybe he can study enough to become a skilled worker, find Marija a job in the plant, and move the family into the neighborhood. But nine days after he begins work, he is laid off.

Embittered by this latest blow, Jurgis at first gives up; but the need for money to survive puts him out on the street again. Day after day he has to fight for a job, for a place to stay warm, even for a spot in a police station to sleep. Only the small amounts of money from the children keep him going. When he does go home, he discovers that he has a chance for a job.

It has come about through a settlement worker who talks to Elzbieta's surviving crippled son at Mike Scully's dump. Like other hungry children he looks for food there, a practice his mother objects to until she finds the scraps are not spoiled because of the cold weather. The young woman calls on Elzbieta, as she has promised the boy, and asks many more questions. Sympathetic to the family's condition, she sends them food and a letter for Jurgis to take to her fiancé, who is superintendent at a steel mill.

Twice as far away as the harvester works, the steel mill is an awesome place to Jurgis, at first because of its appearance in early morning and the hundreds of workers who enter the gates. A subordinate of the superintendent eventually takes him on a tour of the mill to find an opening. From the Bessemer furnace, blast furnaces, and rolling mills to where steel rails for railroad tracks are made, Jurgis is overwhelmed by the noise and the heat. At this latter place he is offered a job and immediately goes to work. But the cost of getting to work is so high that Jurgis sleeps at a lodging house during the week and goes home only on weekends. He quickly gets used to the work and takes risks like the other men, in spite of the accidents he sees. On the occasion of one such accident, when a man is badly burned in the explosion of a brick furnace, Jurgis suffers burns on one hand in giving assistance and must miss several days of work.

This gives Jurgis a chance to be with his son Antanas. Elzbieta is gone in the early morning scrubbing office floors at one of the packinghouses, and she and Marija spend a great deal of time job hunting. Though hard to control, Antanas is tough and determined in a way that gives Jurgis hope for the boy's future.

By the time he goes back to his job at the steel mill, Marija is working as a beef trimmer in a small packinghouse. It is spring, and the streets are full of water as usual. Jurgis begins to plan again: they will be better prepared for the next winter, and the children can go back to school. Coming home on a Saturday after a heavy rain, he finds a crowd in front of the widow's. He is told that Antanas has drowned in the street.

Commentary

If Ona's death, in the previous section, is the turning point in the plot of the novel, then the drowning of Antanas is only reinforcement of this event. It might even be considered a completion of Ona's death in the sense that it makes complete the destruction of Jurgis's immediate family. As events, the two deaths contrast sharply. Ona is seen growing weaker and more tormented, and her condition is complicated by the premature birth of a second child. On the other hand, the death of Antanas is accidental and unexpected. Ona, from the very start, is said to be small and delicate; her chance of survival seems slim. By contrast, Antanas is tough and determined, his father looking upon him as a fighter.

That Jurgis's circumstances are improving, if only temporarily, at the time his son drowns is certainly an instance of dramatic irony. His lifted morale even causes Jurgis to begin planning for the future, as he does when he is employed at the harvester works. His thoughts include what he wants to do for the children.

Sinclair shows the differences between working conditions in the yards and those of Jurgis's new jobs, especially at the harvester works. "It had some thought for its employees; its workshops were big and roomy, it provided a restaurant where the workmen could buy good food at cost, it had even a reading room, and decent places where its girl hands could rest; also the work was free from many of the elments of filth and repulsiveness that prevailed at the stockyards." These differences serve two purposes. One is that no matter how good working conditions are Jurgis is still caught in a system which uses him, and discards him, as it chooses. The other is that the new settings make the character of Jurgis more representative of all workingmen, not just those in the meat packing industry. Some of the force of a propaganda novel comes from its ability to depict what is common to many men in the area of experience about which it attempts to shape the reader's opinion.

Another aspect of the effectiveness of such a novel is its ability to simplify. This is to be seen, for example, in characterization. But simplifying can mean quite different things. If Sinclair's novel is compared with another, similar in some ways, like John Steinbeck's *The Grapes of Wrath*, it can be seen that Sinclair's characters are flat and Steinbeck's round. That is, the reader sees Ona and Jurgis and the others largely from the outside, and they are not memorable. On the other hand, the members of the Joad family have a depth and meaning which increases the more the reader contemplates them. Yet, both novels use characters that are similar in kind of experience.

A good example of the flat character is Elzbieta. The reader knows her no better at the end of the novel than he did at the beginning, and she is indistinguishable from other women in Packingtown who hold families together without complaint and against difficult odds. "Elzbieta was one of the primitive creatures: like the angleworm, which goes on living though cut in half; like a hen, which, deprived of her chickens one by one, will mother the last that is left her." This passage could be located in any section of the novel, and it would describe Elzbieta at the time.

It might also be said that a relatively uncomplicated symbolism can add to the single-minded aim of a propaganda novel. The overall jungle symbolism of Sinclair's novel serves this purpose. In this section, Jurgis is shown in the industrial jungle of machines and furnaces. The harvester works is full of machines that produce an almost endless number of parts: one man handles 30,000 a day; another sharpens 3,000 pieces of steel a day; etc. In the steel mill Jurgis is confronted by a setting "where the air shook with deafening thunder, and whistles shrieked warnings on all sides of him at once; where miniature steam engines came pushing upon him, and sizzling, quivering, white-hot masses of metal sped past him, and explosions of fire and flaming sparks dazzled him and scorched his face." And where he works at moving newly formed steel rails "the ingot seemed almost a living thing; it did not want to run this mad course, but it was in the grip of fate, it was tumbled on, screeching and clanking and shivering in protest." Like the ingot, Jurgis is in a world over which he has no control. Indeed, no one man seems to control the machines and the furnaces. Like the packinghouses earlier, these huge plants are "a thing as tremendous as the universe." Just for a man to survive, he must daily do battle.

CHAPTER 22

Summary

Confirming the death of Antanas by observation and by questioning other members of the family, Jurgis leaves the house and starts walking. When his path is blocked by a freight train, on an impulse he climbs aboard. Once he is on the train, Jurgis battles with himself to forget the past, forget his now dead wife and son, and think only of himself. The smells and sights of the country, which he experiences for the first time in three years, lead him off the train.

His first encounter is with a farmer who takes him for a tramp but whose wife sells him some food. After his meal and a sound sleep, he takes a bath in a pool, the first complete one since he left Lithuania, and washes his clothes. The next farmer he approaches for a meal refuses and orders him away, and Jurgis retaliates by uprooting some newly planted peach trees. He is able to arrange for a meal at another farm, as well as a place to sleep in the barn, and the farmer and Jurgis discuss working conditions in the country and the city after Jurgis turns down a job.

Jurgis's life in the country consists of sleeping where he is able to and foraging for food wherever he can find it. Free and on his own, he soon regains his former health and energy. He chooses to join with a group of tramps; and he soon learns all their tricks. He also meets other men like himself who are looking for whatever work they can find, including that of harvesting. In Missouri, Jurgis joins a harvest crew and works long hours for two weeks. Like the others, he spends his money on liquor and a woman when he is paid. Though ashamed of himself, he moves on and soon recovers his sense of well being.

Jurgis can never completely submerge his conscience — or his memory. When he is spending the night at the home of a newly arrived White Russian immigrant, the sight of the mother bathing her young son so moves Jurgis that he breaks down and hurriedly leaves the house. He hides himself in a woods and weeps in despair.

Commentary

Jurgis's leaving Chicago for the summer is the natural consequence of the deaths of Ona and Antanas. Determined to obliterate his past and concern himself only with his own survival, Jurgis turns, though by chance, to the country, which was his customary environment in Lithuania. The city has meant only frustration, ruined hopes, and suffering. On the other hand, Jurgis feels free and alive outside the city. But the freedom which Jurgis is to have is precisely defined by the fact that these few months are the only time he is ever outside Chicago.

Even this freedom is qualified. Sinclair speaks several times of the "stern system of nature" which makes some men the casual laborers of the world, which makes prostitutes go wherever they are able to exist, and which allows only the strong of either group to survive. Fleeing from the unjust law of society, Jurgis encounters this "stern system." It is always a matter of survival, and the odds are against the individual. Like Huck Finn, Jurgis will have to return to society, though it is evil and inflicts suffering. The only hope, as Sinclair sees it at the end of the novel, is to restructure that society.

This period in the life of Jurgis is characterized by the struggle within him between self-interest and conscience. As he travels on the train out of Chicago, he rejects the life he has so far lived. "He had wasted his life, he had wrecked himself, with his accursed weakness; and now he was done with it—he would tear it out of him, root and branch! There should be no more tears and no more tenderness; he had had enough of them—they had sold him into slavery! Now he was going to be free, to tear off his shackles, to rise up and fight." This echoes very closely the advice he gets from Jack Duane, earlier in the novel. But conscience and memory will not let him alone. "What terror to see what he had been and now could never be— to see Ona and his child and his own dead self stretching out their arms to him, calling to him across a bottomless abyss—and to know that they were gone from him forever, and he writhing and suffocating in the mire of his own vileness!" It may be that the nicety of Jurgis's conscience is a little difficult to believe in a character whose impact on the reader lies in his being a typical working man. Sinclair may have contributed more of himself to the character than is desirable for the sake of verisimilitude.

Sinclair emphasizes the contrast between the settings of country and city. The pleasures of country air and sunlight, the joy of being able to bathe, the satisfaction in moving by oneself and not among a throng of people—all these conditions of Jurgis's short-lived freedom contrast vividly with the harvester works and especially the steel mills, where he last worked. An individual is able to regain, not just his sense of self in this country setting but also his good health and flow of energy. Jurgis even finds himself singing as he goes.

CHAPTERS 23-24

Summary

With the coming of colder weather in early fall, Jurgis returns to Chicago, riding freight trains to get there and determined to use all his knowledge to survive. Neither the steel mill nor the harvester works has a job for him, but through a newspaper advertisement he finally gets work digging on a series of tunnels for telephone lines. Only much later does he learn that these are in fact railway freight subways built, through deception, to ruin the teamsters' and other unions.

Jurgis arranges for room and board as well as clothes and tools. His decision not to buy an overcoat puts him at a disadvantage in the cold weather, making the saloon an even greater necessity. For Jurgis and others like him, saloons are the only places they can go when not working; and they offer a kind of home, with someone to talk to, games to play, and tabloid newspapers to read. However, after only a few weeks on the job, Jurgis breaks his arm. He spends two weeks in the county hospital, including Christmas, and enjoys his stary, except for having to eat canned meat.

Though he is unable to work, Jurgis is released from the hospital. His room is rented, the keeper of the boarding house will not extend him credit, and he has little pay coming from the company he worked for. In short, he is out on the streets in very cold weather without the means to survive. The cold forces him to spend some of his money at a series of saloons just to keep warm. He has no luck in getting accepted as a sitter, one who is allowed "to sit by the fire and look miserable to attract custom." But he does learn of a revival meeting that evening, and he manages to fight his way in with hundreds of others like himself. Though he is there to keep warm, Jurgis is angered by the sermon, which is delivered by a man who is adequately fed and clothed. Such men, he concludes, are part of the reason why workingmen have little chance in the world. After the meeting, he fails to get into a police station to spend the night and is forced to go to a lodging house.

At last, Jurgis has to beg. His practice is to get money and immediately return to a saloon. Under the circumstances, there is no place else that offers him what a saloon does. But he is not a successful beggar. Though his plight is real, he has neither the skill nor the sense of drama the professional beggar has. The longer he is forced to beg, the more Jurgis is filled with bitterness. Every avenue in society is closed to him, and his very existence seems to be a threat to those with wealth and power.

One evening when he is desperately trying to beg among crowds of theater goers, Jurgis encounters a young man whose drunken condition causes them to fall into a conversation of misunderstanding. Jurgis attempts to recount his problems, but the young man wants to talk about his own, including the small allowance his father gives him and his girl friend. When he does realize Jurgis has no home, the young man, Freddie Jones, invites him to come home and have supper with him. When Freddie decides to call a cab, he takes out an amount of money larger than Jurgis has ever seen before. Though Jurgis is tempted to grab the money and run, he does not do so; and Freddie gives him a hundred dollar bill to pay the cab fare. When the cab is hailed, the driver tries to stop Jurgis from getting in, and Freddie has to intervene. With Freddie asleep during the ride, Jurgis again resists the temptation to steal.

The house to which they are taken is a large mansion on Lake Shore Drive. Jurgis cannot even believe it is a private home; but he follows Freddie in, only to be further amazed at the size and decorations of the interior. The butler is hostile to Jurgis from the start and tries to remove him from the house, but Freddie stops him. Young Jones first shows Jurgis the dining room, another marvel he can hardly believe. In conversation, it is revealed that Freddie is the son of Jones the packer and that Jurgis has worked for him. Freddie makes much of this and tries to introduce Jurgis to the butler. After describing the showplace features of the house and their cost, Freddie leads Jurgis upstairs to his apartment, where they are to have supper.

Its decorations are partly collegiate and partly sporting, and it is inhabited by a large bulldog. Jurgis is very uncomfortable in such surroundings, and is made more so by a retinue of servants, under the butler's direction, who lay out the cold supper and wine. Freddie encourages Jurgis to sit down and to eat and drink; and he does so avidly, much to the young host's pleasure. Freddie entertains him with stories about current problems in the family until he falls asleep. The butler, who Jurgis suspects has been waiting in the hall all along, enters soon after and orders Jurgis out of the house. Jurgis refuses to be searched downstairs, and the butler retaliates by giving him a kick as he passes out the front door.

Commentary

The scene between Jurgis and Freddie Jones is one of few long dramatic scenes in the novel, longer even than the confrontation between Jurgis and Ona (Chapters 13-15). And it is as unsatisfactory as the earlier one, though for different reasons. In this encounter between workingman and owner's son, the whole point of the scene is undermined by the fact that it is a coincidence, and an unlikely one. In short, Sinclair is so concerned to underscore his theme that he fails to be convincing. Not even a propaganda novelist can afford to ignore completely the expectations a reader has for a work of fiction.

Sinclair is more convincing when he describes Jurgis's developing, or perhaps repetitious, thoughts about his relationship to society. "He saw the world of civilization then more plainly than ever he had seen it before; a world in which nothing counted but brutal might, an order devised by those who possessed it for the subjugation of those who did not. He was one of the latter; and all outdoors, all life, was to him one colossal prison, which he paced like a pent-up tiger, trying one bar after another, and finding them all beyond his power." Yet even these are obviously Sinclair's words, Sinclair's point of view. But the frustration suggested is everywhere a part of the character he creates to carry his theme.

Sinclair is even more convincing as he depicts the reaction of Jurgis to the evangelists whose warm hall the beggars, bums, and unemployed take advantage of. Listening to the sermon, Jurgis is annoyed. "What did he know about sin and suffering—with his smooth, black coat and his neatly starched collar, his body warm, and his belly full, and money in his pocket—and lecturing men who were struggling for their lives, men at the death-grapple with the demon powers of hunger and cold!" As a character, Jurgis is capable of seeing such an incongruity; and at the same time, the incongruity illustrates well the theme Sinclair is developing.

Sinclair is even more convincing still in presenting the idea of the saloon as the only institution serving such men as Jurgis. When Jurgis begs money, he takes it immediately to a saloon because it can provide what he needs: warmth, a drink, free lunch with the drink, and companionship. The respectable person from whom he gets money cannot understand this because he has other institutions to satisfy his needs. Even when Jurgis is working, the saloon still provides those things which the respectable have in homes or clubs. As Sinclair points out, perhaps partly as a matter of personal bias, the workingman can avail himself of what the saloon provides only on one condition: that he buy a drink and that he continue to buy drinks at acceptable intervals. The price of admission to the workingman's club may be more than the price of drinks; it may be dependency on liquor. Of course, the point is that he has no real choice: either the saloon or freezing to death; either the saloon or losing all chance for companionship.

The symbolism of the jungle is continued in the imagery in this section. The world of begging, like the world of prison, is a veritable jungle. It is a fiercely competitive world with high stakes; an amateur like Jurgis has little chance for anything but survival among professionals to whom it is a profitable business. Then, too, in a passage quoted earlier Jurgis is described as a "pent-up tiger" pacing the small world in which he is confined. If the imagery is animal, it is appropriate to a theme which asserts that society has reduced the workingman to less than human status.

CHAPTERS 25-26

Summary

Though angry at being evicted from the Jones mansion by the butler, Jurgis is more concerned with another problem: he has the hundred dollar bill, but in order to pay for a night's lodging he will have to get it changed. With great apprehension he finally goes into a saloon deserted of customers and asks the bartender for change. As Jurgis has feared, the man will not believe that a tramp could have so much money and insists on inspecting the bill. Jurgis agrees to buy a glass of beer, but the bartender gives him change for only a dollar. When the bartender refuses to produce the rest of the money, Jurgis throws the glass of beer at him and attacks him. A furious fight ensues, ending only when a policeman clubs him unconscious and drags him off to jail.

When Jurgis is tried the next day, he is unable to convince the judge of the truth of his story and also has to admit to being arrested before. Of course, he does not realize the saloon owner has been paying off the police and the bartender works for the local Democratic party. Once more he is sentenced to the Bridewell. To his surprise he soon encounters Jack Duane. And this time, with his family no longer a matter of worry, Jurgis realizes that the way the men in prison look on the world is also his way. And he intends to join Duane as soon as his sentence is up.

Upon release, Jurgis finds Duane in a hideout, after first going to the room of Duane's mistress whose address he has been given. After briefing Jurgis on criminal activity in the city, Duane takes him along on their first job, a strong-arm robbery. Later, after disposing of the victim's jewelry to a fence located within the hideout, Duane divides the loot with Jurgis. Details of the victim's injuries in the newspaper they read the next day upset Jurgis, but Duane argues that it is every man for himself and the victim was probably doing harm to someone else.

Through Duane's conversation and his introduction of Jurgis to the places frequented by important criminals of all kinds, Jurgis learns the inner workings of the alliance between businessmen, politicians, and criminals. At stake is power, and the means to gain or hold power is money. For a man who is accepted at some level in this alliance, there is both money and privilege. Jurgis learns this through Duane's introducing him to a man named "Buck" Halloran. Halooran lets him in on a scheme by which Jurgis is paid to go every Saturday and represent himself as various city laborers in order to collect their pay and turn it over to Halloran. This same man gets Jurgis off with a suspended fine when he starts a fight after getting drunk at a ball given in honor of a well known character who plays violin in a brothel.

Jurgis takes advantage of every opportunity that comes his way. On one occasion he and Duane, assisted by the bartender, follow an out-of-town buyer out of a saloon, rob him of his money and watch, hurry back into the saloon through a basement door, and disappear by using a next-door brothel with many exits, a convenience used to get rid of customers and girls in an emergency. The ensuing friendship of the bartender leads to an introduction to a Jew who works in a brothel and who is looking for someone to beat up a gambler who has caused him trouble. Jurgis is told his pay for such a job would be tips on the races. It is by this means that he learns of the racing trust and the way it controls horse racing for its own benefit. Jurgis and Duane discover that the Jew's tips on the races are good, but the job turns out to be unnecessary.

The coming of the city elections and Halloran's political affiliations interest Jurgis in politics, and he becomes a Democrat like Halloran. When Duane is caught cracking a safe and is almost made an example of in an outraged wave of reform, Jurgis decides to get into politics. His chance comes through "Bush" Harper, the man who helped him become a citizen and who is still working at Brown's, though in reality spying on the unions for the packers. Harper, one of Mike Scully's lieutenants, explains a complicated scheme in which Scully is giving the Democratic nomination for alderman to a rich Jewish brewer and has an agreement with the Republicans to finance their campaign from the brewer's money if they will nominate a friend of Scully's and if they will nominate no candidate at all the following year when Scully himself comes up for re-election as alderman. Since Scully fears that Democrats in the stockyards are angry about the rich brewer's nomination and might bolt the party and even vote for the nominee of the recently appearing Socialist Party instead of the innocuous candidate he has suggested for the Republicans and since the Republicans have no skill in getting nominees elected, there is an urgent need for someone familiar with the yards to organize the Republicans' campaign. Jurgis accepts; and after approval from Scully he is sent to Durham's to be given a job. Of course, Jurgis has no idea that Scully is controlled by the packers.

Working as a hog trimmer, Jurgis joins the union and begins arousing interest in Doyle, the Republican candidate. Jurgis's job is to get new members for the Doyle Republican Association and manage the meetings and rallies. Jurgis is so scrupulous with money that he annoys his fellow workers until he understands that everyone will get a share. On election day he works hard at buying votes in the customary style; and Doyle is elected, everyone mistakenly thinking it a triumph of the people over a capitalist.

Following the election, Jurgis continues to work at Durham's, partly because Scully tells him something important will happen soon. He joins a group of bachelors who enjoy going out on the town; Jurgis can afford entertainment now. He learns very shortly what Scully was talking about: the possibility of a strike. In the new contract with the packers, the union is asking that the wage for unskilled men be established. In spite of increases in the price of dressed meat and decreases in the cost of cattle, the packers are adamant in their refusal of the union demand, in part because thousands of unemployed are available in the city. The result is that the union calls a strike in Chicago and the other large packing centers.

When Jurgis goes to see Scully about a job during the strike, he is told that he should keep the job he has and get as much as he can out of it and that in any case the strike will collapse soon. This startles Jurgis because Scully has publicly criticized the packers. But Jurgis goes back to work as a scab and is welcomed at Durham's. He discovers that though the strikers and the many police assigned to the yards do not want violence the newspapers distort events for the sake of sensation. When he and some friends go outside the gate for a drink and a minor scuffle ensues with a group of strikers, newspaper headlines make the incident into a scene of mob violence.

Very soon, Jurgis is put in charge of the killing beds, a critical operation in the plant because fresh meat at least must be supplied by the packers to those who form public opinion. Assured of a job after the strike is over, Jurgis takes on the impossible task of organizing a crew of criminals, "the lowest foreigners," and "stupid black Negroes." In spite of added comforts, many of the crew work little or not at all. In fact, some discover that they can take jobs in different parts of the plant and make more money. Though Jurgis tries to get the work done, he soon gives up and stops worrying, even accepting bribes from men he catches working at more than one job. From the packers' point of view they feel fortunate if only the diseased and injured animals are killed. All the while, representatives of the plants are rounding up more employees, Negroes from the South and the inhabitants of jails in many cities; and the packers are laying in supplies for the scabs.

In spite of these preparations, the packers give in and allow arbitration. An agreement is reached, and the packers say they will accept union men back on the job. In fact, the packers agree among themselves not to accept union leaders. When the men return to work and this discrimination becomes obvious, anger rises; and soon the strike is back on again.

This time violence is in the air, though the amount of actual violence is exaggerated by the newspapers and is less than that of previous strikes before unions were formed. This time, too, the packers are determined to replace the striking workers. They house the new employees, mainly Southern Negroes, in the plants, though this is against the law. They allow gambling and turn their backs on the fights, drinking, and promiscuity apparent everywhere. The fact that thousands of people are living in a place which normally is unpleasant makes for intolerable conditions. Jurgis is a part of this; because he does not like the role of scab he drinks too much and is bad-tempered.

He and his crew are called out one day when some steers get loose and the strikers butcher them. With other crews and the police, they rush out to punish the offenders. In the general fight, Jurgis and two policemen chase some men into a saloon, and use the occasion to steal money and liquor. Later in the day, after an evening of gambling and drinking, Jurgis unexpectedly encounters Connor again. Once more, he tries to kill the man. Once more, he is beaten senseless and taken off to the police station.

The next day Jurgis calls on Bush Harper to help him, but he comes only after Jurgis's bond is set. But Jurgis has an even greater problem: Harper tells him Connor is high up with Mike Scully. Harper finally agrees to get Jurgis's bail reduced if Jurgis will give him all the money he has to cover it. Then, Jurgis can quickly get out of town. What Harper does not tell Jurgis is that the money will end up in his own pocket. Jurgis accepts the offer, is freed, and goes to another part of the city.

Commentary

The settings into which Sinclair puts Jurgis in this section appear to be quite different from those of the various places he has worked so far. Succeeding as a partner of Duane or in the employ of Mike Scully is a matter of taking advantage of opportunities, demonstrating loyalty, and remaining habitually suspicious of everyone. In both cases, Jurgis feels that he has more control of his destiny and is an insider in his knowledge. In fact, this is not true at all.

Mike Scully is a good indicator of the relationship of Jurgis to these settings. To Jurgis, Scully is a "mighty power" who is able to give orders to the packers or to grant enormous favors to an individual. What Jurgis does not know is that in reality "Scully was but a tool and puppet of the packers" and if he is an alderman he is elected only at the pleasure of his masters. There is more that Jurgis does not know; were he to have such knowledge, he might act as he invariably does toward Connor. "It was Scully who owned the brickyards and the dump and the ic pond. . . . It was Scully who was to blame for the unpaved str in which Jurgis's child had been drowned; it was Scully who I put into office the magistrate who had first sent Jurgis to jai was Scully who was principal stockholder in the company wl had sold him the ramshackle tenement, and then robbed hir it." Scully is rewarded because his abilities serve the purp of his masters, and his rewards are exactly calculated and never be greater. In turn, Scully rewards Jurgis for his faitl ness and ability to work hard, and these rewards will never penny more than is necessary.

In short, Jurgis is used. He has only so much control his own destiny as Scully or one of his lieutenants allows; knows only so much as it is necessary for him to know in orde be useful. He is no more his own man than when he v shoveling guts at Brown's, working when he was told to, ceiving whatever pay the packers chose to give him, and bei turned away when someone else took his place. He is better o committing robberies with Duane or buying votes for Scully in that he has money for food, clothing, shelter, and even entertainment.

In other words, the settings of the criminal world or the world of politics are no different from that of legitimate business.

The fact that this is so reinforces Sinclair's theme in the novel. Society is deeply corrupt, and the ordinary individual is at the mercy of those who manipulate it for their own ends. The picture drawn of the alliance between business, politics, and crime makes clear that nothing short of a transformation of society will make it possible for a man to count.

Historically, Sinclair exaggerates but little in his description of life in Chicago in the early 1900s. And what is true of Chicago is true of other cities during the same period. "The city, which was owned by an oligarchy of business men, being nominally ruled by the people, a huge army of graft was necessary for the purpose of effecting the transfer of power." What is at stake is power; in a capitalist society, Sinclair says, everything has a price. A man's vote is worth three or four dollars depending on how close an election may be. And, of course, the "army of graft" must be maintained. "The leaders and organizers were maintained by the business men directly — aldermen and legislators by means of bribes, party officials out of the campaign funds, lobbyists and corporation lawyers in the form of salaries, contractors by means of jobs, labor union leaders by subsidies, and newspaper proprietors and editors by advertisements. The rank and file, however, were either foisted upon the city, or else lived off the populace directly."

The account of the strike is based on that of 1904 led by the Amalgamated Meat Cutters and Butcher Workmen. The result of the historical strike was that the level of packinghouse wages in 1904 continued to prevail until 1916. In the novel, Sinclair describes some of the reasons why this was so: deception of the packers in negotiating with the union; rebuilding their work force by flooding the labor market and then exercising selection; and steadily increasing prices on dressed meat while forcing down the cost of cattle. Then, too, unions did not have the strong bargaining position which they since have established. This relatively weak position was further complicated in the meat packing industry by the fact that almost all jobs could be performed by unskilled labor. The various stages of meat processing had been broken down into comparatively simple operations requiring little skill from the worker; also, these operations were organized on an assembly line basis. Both of these developments allowed for as much turnover in the work force as the packers desired. From the point of view of the workers, a strong union was difficult to build and maintain in the face of these conditions. The worker's position then is reflected now in the difficulty packinghouse employees have had in finding jobs in other industries as the result of large processing plants closing in recent years. Jobs requiring simple skills but bringing good wages (as the result of long union activity) are hard to come by; retraining is often necessary. Widespread automation in assembly line industries has also had an effect on the nature of the labor force required.

A good example of the extensive use of summary narrative in the novel is the way in which Sinclair handles the appearance of the scabs or strikebreakers in the plants. Little use is made of scenes in which individuals reveal themselves by the way they talk or act. Instead, Sinclair describes group characteristics and group behavior in summary fashion. The picture he gives of the way in which blacks work, eat, sleep, sing, gamble, drink, and fight cannot help but make the reader compare them with the cattle and hogs in nearby pens. The justification for suggesing this parallel might be that the packers treat the black scabs exactly as they do the animals. Further, it might be said that the packers can do this only because the capitalistic system allows them such license.

However, the descriptions Sinclair writes of the strikebreakers raise a question of his own attitude. "As very few of the better class of workingmen could be got for such work, these specimens of the new American hero contained an assortment of the criminals and thugs of the city, besides Negroes and the lowest foreigners — Greeks, Roumanians, Sicilians, and Slovaks. They had been attracted more by the prospect of disorder than by the big wages. . . ." The question is raised by the fact that Sinclair does not clearly attribute the feelings expressed here to the *packers* alone. His passages on the black strikebreakers are even more ambiguous as to his motives. "The ancestors of these black people had been savages in Africa; and since then they had been chattel slaves, or had been held down by a community ruled by the traditions of slavery. Now for the first time they were free—free to gratify every passion, free to wreck themselves." And Sinclair's motives are not clarified when he momentarily puts this group into a scene. "And then at night, when this throng poured out into the streets to play—fighting, gambling, drinking and carousing, cursing and screaming, laughing and singing, playing banjoes and dancing! They were worked in the yards all the seven days of the week, and they had their prize-fights and crap games on Sunday nights as well; but then around the corner one might see a bonfire blazing, and an old, gray-headed Negress, lean and witchlike, her hair flying wild and her eyes blazing, yelling and chanting of the fires of perdition and the blood of the 'Lamb,' while men and women lay down upon the ground and moaned and screamed in convulsions of terror and remorse."

If the attitude toward black people as shown in these passages is that of Sinclair himself, how can it be explained? It may be said that he displays no more ignorance and lack of understanding than anyone else at the turn of the century. But the corollary is also true: he shows no insight into and appreciation of black people and black culture. It is true that Sinclair was born in Baltimore of southern parents and that the blacks he depicts are southern blacks. But it is also true that he was a Socialist at the time he wrote the novel and dedicated it "To the Working-men of America." It is deceptively easy to judge the past in contemporary terms, but it is also possible to expect thinking men at any time to resist following the crowd.

CHAPTERS 27-28

Summary

Though free, Jurgis is cut off from the advantages of belonging to Scully's political machine; and in addition to having no money he suffers from the lack of those material comforts he has gotten used to. It is a bad time to be looking for a job; the large number of unemployed is soon increased by the strike-breakers in the yards, many of whom are replaced by regular workers when the strike fails. Haunted by the prospect of starvation, Jurgis is forced to buy stale bread, rummage through garbage cans, and even steal a cabbage from a produce market in his anger over not being strong enough to keep a job he is given. Like others in his state, he frequents a soup kitchen financed by a newspaper and buys a place to sleep in a stale-beer saloon.

The fact that a presidential election campaign is in full swing makes Jurgis even more mindful of what he has lost. On one occasion, after begging a meal from an old lady, he attends a political rally, not just because the weather is cold but because it reminds him of his former connections. His nostalgia is more painful when he discovers that the speaker is a senator who had earlier addressed the Doyle Republican Association. Though Jurgis tries hard to follow the speech on protective tariffs in order not to fall asleep and snore, he does so and is soon thrown out of the hall. With no money and nowhere to go, Jurgis starts begging again; and his first subject turns out to be a woman who had been at his wedding feast. From her he learns Marija's whereabouts, and in a surge of homesickness he goes to find her.

No sooner has Jurgis arrived at the large house to inquire about Marija than the police rush in. In the ensuing panic, he hurries about with the men and women he discovers in the house, trying one exit after another, finding them all blocked by the police. The house is a brothel, and it is being raided by the police. Jurgis finds Marija, and when the police order them to dress and get ready to go she takes him to her room with her. He is saddened that Marija is a prostitute but realizes his own life has not been more decent. From her he learns of the family: Stanislovas has been killed by rats; Elzbieta is working when she can, with Marija providing money to keep the children in school; Tamoszius has lost a finger and can no longer play the violin. Marija tells Jurgis that no one blames him for running away after his son's death, though she now thinks the family's problems could have been avoided if Jurgis had let Ona continue with Connor. When everyone is rounded up to be taken outside and then to the police station, Jurgis tells Marija he is wanted by the police. Marija has the madame try to intercede with the police, but it does no good and Jurgis must go along with the others.

In jail, Jurgis thinks over what has happened to the family and how far they are from his old hopes and dreams. He has tried to shut all this out of his mind, but old feelings have caught him unexpectedly.

In the morning Jurgis appears in court, the same court in which earlier his sentence for fighting has been suspended. Jurgis is eventually dismissed, though not with the men who are clients of the brothel, and the women are fined. Jurgis returns to the house with Marija, and she tells him of her life there. She has become addicted to the morphine which is commonly given to women when they first come to a brothel. Another trick to keep the women from leaving, besides taking their clothes away, is to let them run up debts, since they are charged for their room and services. Marija cites several examples of women who have been deceived into becoming prostitutes and kept at it by various tricks. After hearing the story of Jurgis's life for the past year, Marija offers to help him until he finds a job. After lunch together, Marija sends him off to find Elzbieta.

But Jurgis is reluctant to face Elzbieta until he is employed. After a dinner paid for by the money Marija gave him, he decides impulsively to go to a meeting in the same hall from which he was ejected the previous night. Paying little attention to events on the platform, Jurgis worries about how Elzbieta will receive him. Again, he falls asleep; again, he fights to stay awake. He is startled by a woman's voice encouraging him to listen. When he is able to watch her, he sees she is beautiful and cultivated; even more, she is transfixed by the words of the person speaking. Having been an insider in politics, Jurgis cannot understand this reaction to the kind of planned show he himself used to help organize. He then turns to observe the speaker and encounters first a pair of eyes that are disturbing to look at and then a powerful voice. Jurgis feels the speaker is talking directly to him.

The speaker evidently has been describing the ways in which society and man's life can be changed for the better. Jurgis begins to listen as the speaker says that though those in the audience may not believe yet in what he has described, he will go on saying it again and again until they do for he represents the millions who are oppressed and miserable. He calls especially on workingmen whose labors have built this society but whose voice is not heard. He has been one of them, has suffered the slavery they suffer; he knows what it costs a workingman to gain knowledge, for he himself has paid the price. He is certain his message will reach someone in the audience and enlightenment will set such a man free.

He calls upon workingmen to understand what the war then being fought in Manchuria means in human terms: men killing each other without reason. But if this is too far away to seem real, he calls attention to the injustice and misery forced upon thousands in their own city of Chicago, men, women, and children. And he describes how the labor and suffering of these many thousands serve only the purpose of allowing the few to lead lives of idleness and luxury. These are the few who own not only the people but the government as well. He asks if it is these who will break the slavery of the workingman, who will lead him out of despair and hopelessness. No, only the workingman himself can do this, slowly and against every kind of restraint; only the workingman joining with others like him can accomplish this revolution. Once banded together, workingmen will be an irresistible force.

Jurgis leaps to his feet and shouts with the rest of the audience. The speaker has touched his old dreams and desires; what Jurgis has given up as impossible is reawakened before his very eyes. He does not need to accept defeat.

Commentary

It is significant that the two main settings in this section are a brothel and a Socialist rally. The one is a symptom of the sickness of a capitalistic society: there are the users and the used, and the pleasure that is bought there is at the expense of women who are deceived and coerced into letting their bodies be used or who must trade their bodies for the means to survive. Sinclair's asceticism is obvious in his depiction of life in a brothel, but in the main his purpose is to use that life as an example of the oppression the Socialist orator later describes. It is but one of the conditions of slavery against which the speaker urges workingmen to revolt. The two settings are also an appropriate base for what happens in the novel on the level of plot and characterization as well as theme.

As for plot, Marija's being in a brothel is parallel to Jurgis's inability to hold the job he is offered. With the death of Ona and Antanas, Jurgis's life has moved steadily downhill, in spite of his momentarily improved standard of living while with Duane or working for Mike Scully. And Marija has become a prostitute because there is no other way to support herself and help Elzbieta with the children. But soon after Jurgis leaves Marija in the brothel, he enters the hall where a Socialist rally is being held. At a low point in the life of all of them, he encounters that which will affect him profoundly. At the end of the speech he is said not to be quite the same man. In light of the way the plot of the novel is developed, this is unexpected and hardly prepared for. Ona's death, followed by that of Antanas, has been the turning point in the plot. Socialism has briefly been mentioned only twice before, most recently during Jurgis's work for the Doyle Republican Association. The effect, then, is of a second turning point, but one which applies only to Jurgis, as will be shown later on. And as the last section of the novel also demonstrates, perhaps not intentionally, Socialism is still only a hope, a promise, not a reality, for Jurgis.

On the level of characterization, marked changes are shown in Marija and forecast for Jurgis. She shocks Jurgis by the view of life she has gained from her experience. "When people are starving . . . and they have anything with a price, they ought to sell it, I say. I guess you realize it now when it's too late. Ona could have taken care of us all, in the beginning." Her vitality, her optimism have gone; and her disillusioned knowledge that everything has a price is a perfect reflection of the system which has victimized her. In part, Jurgis is shocked because he himself has lived by the same view while working for Scully, accepted it without thinking until once more he is tossed aside by the system. In vivid contrast to Marija, who will never leave the brothel, is Jurgis at the conclusion of the Socialist orator's speech. "All that he had ever felt in his whole life seemed to come back to him at once, and with one new emotion, hardly to be described. That he should have suffered such oppressions and such horrors was bad enough; but that he should have been crushed and beaten by them, that he should have submitted, and forgotten, and lived in peace – ah, truly that was a thing not to be put into words, a thing not to be borne by a human creature, a thing of terror and madness!" Jurgis has been touched by an idea; and ideas, once conveyed, have endless and irreversible consequences.

As for theme, Jurgis's moving from brothel to rally indicates a shift from depicting the workingman victimized by society or the system to showing Socialism as the means by which workingmen can unite in order to profoundly change that society. As was the case on the level of plot, this shift in theme is unexpected. Its only justification may be that to this point Sinclair has documented the reasons why society must be changed. Such a justification may be acceptable on the level of propaganda; it is less acceptable on the level of the usual expectations a reader has of a novel. For a novel, the change in theme comes too late.

The speaker Jurgis hears is talking about change and the justification for it. In the next and final section, Jurgis will hear a long conversation on Socialist doctrine and practices. Here, the speaker pinpoints the need for a radical change in society by describing the position of the "masters." "They own not merely the labor of society, they have bought the governments; and everywhere they use their raped and stolen power to intrench themselves in their privileges, to dig wider and deeper the channels through which the river of profits flows to them!" The key to change is the enlightened workingman, who bands with his fellows to become "the voice of Labor." Once this enlightenment occurs, nothing can ever deceive him again. "The scales will fall from his eyes, the shackles will be torn from his limbs—he will leap up with a cry of thankfulness, he will stride forth a free man at last!"

Though Jurgis is moved by the speaker, the eloquence is in the situation rather than in the words. Sinclair gives the speaker an imagery as threadbare as that of his own narrative style. The "fierce wolves" and "ravening vultures," the "river of profits," the "flash of lightning," the "scales" and "shackles" of the previous quotations are hardly real eloquence, though a speech has persuasive qualities the written word cannot have. And it does not help much that wolves and vultures echo the symbol of the jungle, as imagery elsewhere does. Sinclair could be a better propagandist and a better novelist in this book if he had an ear for language.

CHAPTERS 29-31

Summary

Filled with a sense of freedom, Jurgis cannot understand why the rest of the meeting is necessary: comments by the chairman, a collection, a question and answer period with the speaker. Jurgis desperately wants to be a comrade with someone but realizes he looks like a tramp. With his new feelings, he does not want to leave the meeting; and he goes in search of the speaker, now backstage. The man recognizes that Jurgis wants to learn about Socialism and, after questioning him, turns him over to a Comrade Ostrinski. Eventually taking Jurgis home with him, Ostrinski has Jurgis tell him his history and then explains his own circumstances. He and his wife are "pants-finishers," making less and less money all the time because it is an easy job for others to learn.

Ostrinski uses his own position as a workingman to explain Socialism to Jurgis. One purpose of Socialism is to make workers class conscious: to get them to see that all they have to sell is their labor while capitalists have money, property, and power.

The result of class conscious workers will be the opportunity to control the government by elections and end "private property in the means of production." Labor unions have failed because in the so-called competitive system owners can also organize. Ostrinski goes on to explain to Jurgis the way the Socialist Party is organized and the fast pace at which it is growing. Ostrinski, a Pole, was earlier involved in the workers' movement in Europe. Jurgis is overwhelmed by what has been accomplished by people like Ostrinski, but the latter explains that after the first flush of enthusiasm Jurgis will be faced by long, hard work. Ostrinski tells him that the party is absolutely democratic as an organization and that in its dealings with other parts of society it follows the principle of no compromise. He goes on to point out that the Socialists are an international party, rapidly growing in strength and achievement. It is the "new religion of humanity."

From Ostrinski, and later from party literature, Jurgis learns the meaning of his experiences in Packingtown. He sees the packers as the Beef Trust and understands that as a worker he was used no differently from the hogs and cattle. He traces the way this trust controls for its own ends all levels of government and all aspects of business. Only the Socialists will be able to turn the anger of the public at the evils perpetrated by the Beef Trust into the constructive change which will make such trusts impossible.

The next day, Jurgis does finally go to Elzbieta; and though she has no interest in politics she is willing to tolerate Jurgis's talk when she sees his new convictions will make him industrious. Soon after, he finds a job, as porter at a hotel, and is amazed to learn from Ostrinski that the proprietor, Tommy Hinds, is a well-known Socialist. Hinds has had a long career of fighting vested interests and graft. After encountering defective equipment as a soldier in the Civil War and dishonest practices as a new businessman in Chicago, he set out to fight these evils and at last ended up a Socialist. His hotel is a center of political discussion and Socialist propaganda. When Hinds himself is not there, his clerk, a former Kansas farmer who has fought the railroads, carries on the debate for him. If not the clerk, then the

assistant clerk, a New Englander who has been in prison for trying to organize the workers in a South Carolina cotton mill.
Recently, many cattlemen have been stopping at the hotel, short
of money because of the packers' manipulation of prices. Hinds
uses Jurgis to acquaint them with true conditions in the yards.
And when Hinds mentions the Beef Trust and a cattleman speaks
of the public indignation over it, the hotel proprietor points out
that such outcries are really manipulated by all those trusts
which together form the Railroad Trust. What is at stake is control of the entire country, and the adversaries are the Beef Trust
and the Railroad Trust.

Jurgis's education takes place, then, at Hind's hotel. Of
course, his old habits give way slowly; sometimes he has too
much to drink. But soon the newly learned doctrines of Socialism
become his means of intoxication. This makes him very impatient with possible converts. They counter with ideas that private
ownership is more economical and that Socialism is paternalistic.
They are unable to see themselves as anything but wage slaves,
and Jurgis learns that his job will be to work for their conversion
patiently but firmly. He uses every means to educate himself for
the task: Socialist literature, fellow employees, party meetings.
Now that a presidential election campaign is on, he hears many
notable speakers. They include the author of a book on capitalism; a young novelist of varied experience with sympathy for
the poor; a former millionaire, now editor of a magazine, who
explains Socialism in relation to the laws of economic evolution;
and finally the Socialist candidate for president, an ex-union
leader who several years before led his railroad union out in an
unsuccessful strike. Jurgis also becomes familiar with the *Appeal
to Reason,* a Socialist weekly. Published in a small Kansas town,
the paper is a propaganda medium to discredit the opposition
and encourage party members. It is also printing special issues
during the campaign addressed to striking workers. Jurgis assists in delivering copies of such an issue to Packingtown
workers, who have lost the strike. He notices changes there,
especially the increasing strength of the Socialists and the des-
peration of Scully and the Democratic machine. At a meeting
called by the Democrats to make an issue out of the Negro strike

breakers, the Socialists virtually take over; and Jurgis has to be restrained from telling all he knows about Democratic vote buying.

Soon after getting a job, Jurgis calls on Marija to tell her she can now leave the brothel. She refuses, saying she cannot get any other job now and in addition she cannot break her morphine habit. Jurgis is greatly disappointed, just as he is at home, with Elzbieta ill and her sons uncontrollable. Yet, now that ideas are his greatest concern, his life can always be interesting and worthwhile. The evening before the election, Jurgis is exposed to a memorable discussion of Socialist ideas.

The occasion is made possible by a millionaire who has devoted his life to settlement work. To his home in the slums he has invited, among others, an Eastern magazine editor skeptical of Socialism; and he asks Jurgis to come, possibly to speak about his experiences in Packingtown. Jurgis finds that the main conversationalists are Lucas, an itinerant evangelist turned itinerant Socialist speaker, and Nicholas Schliemann, a Swedish ex-professor of philosophy whose living habits are as much determined by a scientific approach as his ideas on politics and economics. Jurgis's entrance has interrupted a discussion between the editor and Schliemann, who resumes his analysis of the real nature of institutions in a way that dazzles the working-man. When Schliemann asserts that religion is used by capitalists to further enslave the workingman, Lucas breaks in to say that this is true of religion as an institution but should not be true of religion as the word of God. He goes on to describe Jesus as the first revolutionary, the first Socialist, one who always opposed the possessors of wealth and power for their own sake and cast his lot with the ordinary man as well as the weak and the outcast.

In answer to the editor's question, Lucas and Schliemann agree that a Socialist believes in two things: "the common ownership and democratic management" of the means of production; "the class-conscious political organization of the wage-earners" as the way by which the first is achieved. They disagree, however, on the nature of the society to emerge as the result of this change. Lucas sees it as the New Jerusalem; Schliemann, as an anarchic society of perfect freedom characterized by association according to interest. In such a society as the latter envisions, one hour's work a day is sufficient because the resources of science would be fully utilized. This is in contrast to the present competitive system which is characterized by waste in every aspect. All of its institutions and activities are brought about by needless competition in acquiring wealth and power. Such competition breeds status-seeking, vice, imitation, and adulteration.

In a cooperative society, with no competition for wealth and power, with no profit motive, the use of capital, an individual's earning and spending, the sale of anything, and even jobs are all a matter of record keeping and universal information. The price of anything, Schliemann explains, is what it costs to make it; naturally, this applies only to material needs. For anything else, those who have a common interest associate in order to support it as well as benefit from it. The new society will also benefit from "the positive economics of co-operation." Science and technology will eliminate drudgery, such as dish-washing, and provide for greatly increased crop production as well as more efficient ways of carrying out such production. Science also demonstrates that meat is unnecessary; and Socialism, setting labor free, will cause unpleasant and dangerous tasks, including the processing of meat, to disappear or be done on an individual basis. The new society will do much to improve the health of all citizens by enabling medical knowledge to be applied so as to prevent disease.

The day after this enlightening evening is election day, and Jurgis, along with the other employees at the hotel, goes to watch the returns at a party gathering. The final Socialist vote across the country is more than three times greater than that in the last presidential election (1900). As each local reports, there is cheering as well as speechmaking. The gains in the city are even greater, and in Packingtown the Socialist vote is close to the Democratic. An orator tells the crowd that Chicago is setting an example for workingmen all over the country but that as party members they must work tirelessly to make all who voted with them real Socialists and to allow nothing to impede a momentum which will cause them to seize control of the city at last.

Commentary

The events and the outcome of the election described in this section are based on the history of the election of 1904. The statistics Sinclair uses are actual ones. The Socialist total was a small percentage of the approximately 13.5 million votes cast, in a population of about 75 million. The Socialist candidate for president, whom Sinclair briefly describes, was Eugene Debs. The election was won by the incumbent president and Republican candidate, Theodore Roosevelt.

Just as the moving speech which Jurgis hears at the end of the previous section marks his first awareness of and conversion to Socialism, so the comments by Schliemann here are a sign of Jurgis's education in party ideas and doctrines. Or, at least, so it may seem. It is to be wondered if Sinclair is not aiming more directly at the reader. During the course of both scenes, Jurgis as a character in the action almost disappears from sight. This is certainly the case in the latter scene. It must be remembered that in a propaganda novel every means is used to convey the message the author has in mind, and he may slight the reader's expectations of fiction to achieve his purpose.

The final events of the plot as shown in this section are meant to indicate that all will go well with Jurgis now that he has found Socialism. Whether or not this proves to be the case in human terms is problematical. Certainly every event in the novel up to this last section demonstrates just the opposite. If, for example, the last section were removed as well as the preceding scene in which Jurgis hears the speech which is meant to change his life, the novel would be quite different. It would then depict the relentless destruction of a man and his family by a system over which he has no control. It is ironical that in doing such a thorough job of showing the conditions which make Socialism the only possible means of change Sinclair makes it impossible to believe that Socialism will save his main character. The only objective evidence is about 3 percent of the vote in an election. Perhaps all Sinclair means to say is that whereas Jurgis was a man without hope now at least he does have that. Strictly on the basis of plot development, this last section is unprepared for, and represents a weakness in the novel.

On the level of characterization, Jurgis undergoes something like a religious experience, as Sinclair describes it. Following the speech at the end of the previous section, Jurgis now examines his new feelings. "He had never been so stirred in his life—it was a miracle that had been wrought in him. He could not think at all, he was stunned; yet he knew that in the mighty upheaval that had taken place in his soul, a new man had been born." This is Saul on the road to Tarsus. Nothing less than a true conversion could explain such a reaction. And it does happen to individuals for many reasons. But to use such an experience in a novel, no matter what kind of novel, requires that the author convince the reader of it. To convince is to show, not just to state. As has been pointed out frequently, too often Sinclair states and summarizes and does not dramatize. When he now wants the reader to believe in his character's conversion, Sinclair has little claim on the reader's ability to believe.

The reference to Socialism as "the new religion of humanity" reinforces the idea of rebirth in the character of Jurgis, and incidentally suggests a new imagery for this section to oppose that of the jungle of the rest of the novel. Another change has come about in him too, accompanying the first. "His outward life was commonplace and uninteresting; he was just a hotel porter, and expected to remain one while he lived; but meantine, in the realm of thought, his life was a perpetual adventure." That he should now be interested solely in ideas is perhaps no harder to believe in than his conversion; but it is no easier, either. The chief demonstration of this change is that he is said to read party literature and is shown listening to discussions of Socialist ideas. As an active participant, Jurgis speaks only of his experiences in the packinghouses and as a buyer of votes for Scully.

The problem of characterization here is really the problem of the propaganda novel. Message is the first concern; but if plot and characters are not believable the message has no more impact than if it were conveyed in an article or essay.

In the development of characters, Jurgis should be compared with Marija and Elzbieta. Marija remains in the brothel, seeing it as her destiny; Elzbieta is ill and has sons who are difficult to control. There is no problem with believing this as the last view of the family of Jurgis. Socialism has not touched them. Of those minor characters first appearing in this section, Sinclair succeeds with Hinds and his clerks but is less convincing with Schliemann, whom Jurgis sees as resembling "a thunderstorm or an earthquake." He more nearly resembles Sinclair, with his abstinence and vegetarianism. Schliemann is a mind and voice rather than a character, a convenient way to get into the story Sinclair's own version of Socialism and the ways it could change the quality of life.

Clearly the theme of the novel in this last section is that Socialism is the only hope for the workingman. Individual effort is ineffective; unions are negated by more powerful owners' associations. Only a basic change in the social order will make it possible for workingmen to gain freedom. And freedom as the result of Socialism is heralded everywhere in this section. Lack of freedom, wage slavery, has been the theme up to this point in the novel. Just as the new directions in plot and characterization in this section are unprepared for, so this new theme comes as a surprise.

The ideas which represent Socialism are attributed to several characters: Tommy Hinds, Ostrinski, Lucas, and Schliemann. There are two aspects of these ideas: one is religious; the other, scientific. The religious aspect depicts Socialism as a panacea, a new religion, or the New Jerusalem. The scientific aspect reveals Socialism as efficient, labor-saving, rational, and orderly. These ideas are also a base for criticism of existing society, and the criticism comes in the form of seeing that in a competitive society (capitalism) wealth and power are at stake. Certainly the frame of reference such ideas represent makes coherent what has been said and shown up to this point, even though the last section may have serious fictional weaknesses.

Schliemann's idea that in a Socialist society "anyone would be able to support himself by an hour's work a day" is reminiscent of that of another and earlier anarchist thinker, Henry David Thoreau. In *Walden,* Thoreau estimated that working six weeks a year would be enough for a man to maintain himself. Like Schliemann, Thoreau lived his ideas experimentally in order to see if they tested by experience. And on a related point there is also an interesting comparison: the matter of value. Thoreau wrote that the value of anything is the amount of a man's life he is willing to spend for it. Schliemann distinguishes between material and intellectual needs: the first should be provided for all men with the least waste in time and labor; the second is a matter of individual choice and cannot be translated into price. In other words, as little of a man's life as possible should have to be spent on material needs. Thoreau's criticism was that a man could spend up his life buying food, clothing, and shelter and never really experience what it was like to be truly a man.

CHARACTERIZATION

In *"The Jungle* as Propaganda," the effect of the purpose of the novel on characterization was discussed. Characterization was said to be illustrative, narrow in range, and external. For these reasons, the four main characters will be treated as a group.

The first view of these characters fixes the range of human nature to be expected by the reader. Jurgis is a big man, his physical strength obvious but his inner resources doubtful. The latter is confirmed by his habitual response of greater effort as the only way to solve problems. Ona is frail, as frightened by marriage as by life, and dependent on Jurgis to see her through whatever may happen in the future. Elzbieta is first shown carrying in food for the feast; she is working and inconspicuous. As Ona's stepmother, she has provided support for the young woman in the past and no doubt will be called upon in the future. Marija is conspicuous indeed, by exercise of will determined to make the feast succeed and to continue even beyond everyone's energy. But even her determination cannot really make it a success. Significantly, she is distinguished by her strength, like Jurgis. Jurgis is the head of this immigrant family; by custom, it will succeed or fail even as he succeeds or fails.

Just as no later view of these characters suggests a greater range of human nature, so their presentation here by external means sets the pattern for the entire novel. When Jurgis says "I will work harder" to solve the problem of the expenses of the feast, the reader has no way of knowing what this means to him in the interior life every man leads or how this affects the image he has of himself as a man. So also, later, when Jurgis sprains his ankle and is unable to work, the despair he is said to face for the first time is put into words that reveal little of what facing starvation means for this individual. It might be any man reacting. Just as Ona's fear of the world in the opening scene is conveyed only by her pallor and nervousness, so later the peculiar humiliation of giving herself to Connor is shown only in the twitching and groveling before Jurgis in their bedroom. Again, the words she says to her husband have no counterpart in the images she has of herself. Later in the novel, Elzbieta is said to be a mother earth figure; but this analogy reveals little more about her than the fact that in this first scene she carries food to the table. And Marija's insistence on the singing and playing of a love song at the feast is about as revealing as her admission to Jurgis toward the end of the novel that she can never give up morphine.

Given that characterization in the novel is narrow in range and external, it is logical that it should also be illustrative. Jurgis's strength is also his weakness; and he goes steadily downhill, amid misfortune after misfortune in his family, until by chance he hears a Socialist speech. Thereafter, his fortunes improve, although he sees himself as a hotel porter the rest of his life. The fragile Ona never has a chance, and in a sense her husband's getting her pregnant is as cruel a blow in her undoing as Connor's unwanted attention. But the oppressive climate of wage slavery is said to wither her spirit. Elzbieta endures one death after another and accepts Jurgis as a Socialist only because he is sober and industrious. Marija, who fights the system in personal combat even when she is a union member, ends up a prostitute, addicted to narcotics and enunciating a philosophy of selling to survive. Ona and Marija are negative illustrations of Socialism as the answer to wage slavery; Jurgis, a partly positive one. Only Elzbieta seems impervious to all systems, like Faulkner's character of Dilsey in *The Sound and the Fury*.

What this analysis suggests is that the four characters discussed are the main characters in *The Jungle* only because they are most important to the story, not because they are conceived or handled differently from the less important ones.

REVIEW QUESTIONS AND THEME TOPICS

1. Try to demonstrate that Sinclair's theme in the novel is apparent or implied in Chapter 1. Be fair in presenting evidence, and do not force things to fit the theme.

2. Assume that the novel ends after Jurgis leaves Marija in the brothel in Chapter 28. Explain why this change would make *The Jungle* a social protest novel.

3. If you do not agree that the change suggested in the preceding question would make *The Jungle* a novel of social protest, then explain why Sinclair's theme would not be affected by the change.

4. In Chapter 27, Marija says, "When people are starving . . . and they have anything with a price, they ought to sell it, I say." Show that this view of life is the product of the wage slavery caused by capitalism as Sinclair depicts such conditions.

5. In Chapter 31, Jurgis is said to realize that he will always be a porter but that he is free to explore "the realm of thought." Analyze this effect of Socialism on Jurgis so as to explain what Sinclair is offering to the individual as an alternative to capitalism.

6. What kind of life could little Antanas have led if he had survived? In your discussion, use the children of Elzbieta as examples or parallels.

7. Use the characters of the Widow Jukniene and Madame Haupt to describe the quality of life in Packingtown.

8. Analyze what Sinclair says of politics in Chicago by tracing Mike Scully's connections with government, business, and crime.

9. From what Nicholas Schliemann says in Chapter 31, describe the outlines of the utopia his version of Socialism would produce.

10. Compare the functions in relation to Jurgis of the characters of Jack Duane and Freddie Jones.

11. Justify Sinclair's inclusion of the tour of the packing-house in Chapter 3. Be clear and specific on the grounds for your justification.

12. From the point of view of plot, why does Sinclair have Jurgis spend a summer in the country (Chapter 22)?

13. Write an essay on the saloon as a social institution for workingmen and a means of survival for the unemployed. Draw in Sinclair's comments from the various places where they appear in the novel.

14. Are Sinclair's arguments against "drink" appropriate to the setting and characters he depicts? Or are they personal and imposed on the story? Present evidence for whichever conclusion you support.

SELECTED BIBLIOGRAPHY

BENSON, PETER. "Possession and Dispossession in Crevecoeur's, Sinclair's, and Dos Passos's America." *Bridges: An African Journal of English Studies* 4 December 1992: 91–112.

BLOODWORTH, WILLIAM A., JR. *Upton Sinclair.* Boston: Twayne Publishers, 1977.

BUITENHUIS, PETER. "Upton Sinclair and the Socialist Response to World War I." *Canadian Review of American Studies* 14.2 (1983): 121–130.

COOK, TIMOTHY. "Upton Sinclair's *The Jungle* and Orwell's *Animal Farm*: A Relationship Explored." *Modern Fiction Studies* 30 (1984): 696–703.

DAWSON, HUGH J. "Winston Churchill and Upton Sinclair: An Early Review of *The Jungle*." *American Literary Realism* 24 (1991): 72–78.

DELL, FLOYD. *Upton Sinclair: A Study in Social Protest.* 1927. New York: George H. Doran, 1969.

DERRICK, SCOTT. "What's a Beating Feel Like: Authorship, Dissolution, and Masculinity in Sinclair's *The Jungle*." *Studies in American Fiction* 23 (1995): 85–100.

FONER, PHILIP S. "Upton Sinclair's *The Jungle*: The Movie." *Upton Sinclair: Literature and Social Reform.* Ed. Dieter Herms. Frankfurt: Peter Lang, 1990. 150–67.

GRENIER, JUDSON A. "Muckraking the Muckrakers: Upton Sinclair and His Peers." *Reform and Reformers in the Progressive Era.* Eds. David R. Colburn and George E. Pozzetta. Westport, Connecticut: Greenwood Press, 1983. 71–92.

HARRIS, LEON. *Upton Sinclair: American Rebel.* New York: Thomas Y. Crowell, 1975.

HERMS, DIETER, ed. *Upton Sinclair: Literature and Social Reform.* Frankfurt: Peter Lang, 1990.

MOOKERJEE, R. N. *Art of Social Justice: The Major Novels of Upton Sinclair.* Metuchen, New Jersey: Scarecrow Press, 1988.

WADE, LOUISE CARROLL. "The Problem with Classroom Use of Upton Sinclair's *The Jungle.*" *American Studies* 32.2 (1991): 79–101.

NOTES

Think Quick

Now there are more Cliffs Quick Review® titles, providing help with more introductory level courses. Use Quick Reviews to increase your understanding of fundamental principles in a given subject, as well as to prepare for quizzes, midterms and finals.

Do better in the classroom, and on papers and tests with Cliffs Quick Reviews.

Legends In Their Own Time

Ancient civilization is rich with the acts of legendary figures and events. Here are three classic reference books that will help you understand the legends, myths and facts surrounding the dawn of civilization.

Cliffs Notes on Greek Classics and *Cliffs Notes on Roman Classics*— Guides to the idealogy, philosophy and literary influence of ancient civilization.

Cliffs Notes on Mythology—An introduction to the study of various civilizations as they are revealed in myths and legends.

Find these legendary books at your bookstore or order them using the form below.